100 Natural Ways To Grow A Church

A Guide To Orthodox Evangelism
In North America

Adam Lowell Roberts

**Forward by
His Grace Bishop JOHN
Diocese of Worcester
and New England**

100 NATURAL WAYS TO GROW A CHURCH
A Guide To Orthodox Evangelism In North America

Copyright © 2015 by Adam Lowell Roberts
All rights reserved.

Scripture quotations are taken from The Orthodox Study Bible, 2008 by Thomas Nelson, Inc. Used by permission.

Published by: CreateSpace Independent Publishing Platform
Printed by: CreateSpace

ISBN-13: 978-1517483876
ISBN-10: 1517483875

Cover design, texts and illustrations:
Copyright © 2015 by Man of War Design
(http://www.manofwardesign.com)

ACKNOWLEDGMENT-

*For many days and nights I have researched
the information in this book at the sacrifice
of time with my wife and children.
This book would not be possible without them.*

"We need this! Every Orthodox parish should have this book and follow its practical suggestions if we are to have a vibrant and growing Orthodox Church in America."
Robert Arakaki
Administrator of OrthodoxBridge.com, A Meeting Place For Evangelicals, Reformed, & Orthodox Christians

"The most urgent missiological need in the Orthodox world today is the need to re-evangelize our own nominal Orthodox people. 'The beautiful feet of those who preach the gospel' will find this book to be an effective guide for keeping the gospel clear and central to that goal, as well as for all non-Orthodox seekers of truth."
Bradley Nassif, Ph.D.
Professor of Biblical and Theological Studies, North Park University (Chicago)

"Adam Roberts has created an amazingly practical and helpful resource. This is exactly what local parishes need to help them reach their communities for Christ."
Deacon Michael Hyatt
New York Times Bestselling Author

"Practicing these with love, prayer, and a humble heart will help you and your church."
Deacon Andrew Bardwell
All Saints Of North America, Homer, Alaska

"May God continue to bless your evangelistic efforts, and may this book help people realize and make real the Great Commission in their parishes and in their lives as Orthodox Christians."
Father Mark Rowe
Dean, ROCOR Western Rite Communities

"Our Lord Jesus Christ called His followers to be light, salt, and yeast in society. In other words, we are to offer a witness of God's Love and Good News to all people everywhere. Too often, though, our Churches remain closed and stagnant, uninterested in sharing our great treasure of faith with those outside our faith community. Even those communities that want to faithfully follow Christ's evangelistic call, often don't know how to do it. This creative little book by Adam Lowell Roberts answers the question "how" by offering 100 practical and easy ideas for a congregation to implement, so that they can take more seriously their role in offering Christ's light to the world around us."
Father Luke A. Veronis
Director of the Missions Institute of Orthodox Christianity

"Creating vibrant communities is our first priority as members of the Body of Christ. The parish is the primary icon of Christ in the world and our local communities. This short book provides clergy and lay members alike simple, direct, and easy to implement ideas that can enliven any community."
Father Evan Armatas
Pastor of St. Spyridon's Greek Orthodox Church, Loveland, Colorado
Host of "Orthodoxy Live" on Ancient Faith Radio

"More years ago than I care to remember, I baptized Adam Roberts. I am happy to see that it has born fruit. Adam's book *One Hundred Natural Ways to Grow A Church* is a handy collection of mostly simple things that can be used for outreach, and we often don't think of. We often think in grandiose terms about Missions and Evangelism—long term planning, exciting programs and spending gobs of money. This has its place, but most local congregations do not have the resources to do them. Adam Roberts' book has suggestions that any congregation can try, and have success with. Get it for your parish library."
Father Michael Keiser
Chairman of the Dept. of Missions & Evangelism for the Antiochian Archdiocese of North America

"Each reader will find many methods of evangelism as presented by Adam Roberts that they can implement both in their parish and in their personal interactions with others."
Father Matthew Howell
Pastor of St. Herman's Antiochian Orthodox Church, Wasilla, Alaska

"Without any organized efforts at evangelism some 23% of Orthodox Christians in the United States are converts. Imagine for a moment what kind of a harvest could be reaped if Orthodox Christians got organized? With the book *100 Natural Ways to Grow A Church,* pastors, missionaries and lay leaders will have a tool that will help Orthodox churches and missions of any size or rite to effectively reach out in an organized manner. Even more importantly, these 100 ways do not come from mere brainstorming, but are currently being used effectively by Orthodox churches of various jurisdictions and rites in the United States. There is something in this book for everyone. I highly recommend it!"
Father Victor Novak
Pastor of Holy Cross ROCOR Orthodox Church in Omaha, Nebraska

"For all of those in Orthodox Christian Churches in America who get the "why" of outreach and evangelism, but are struggling with the "how", Adam Lowell Roberts has put together a wonderfully practical and evidence based resource that is both relevant and easy to use. Thank you, Adam!"
Father Gregory Hohnholt
Pastor of Holy Trinity Greek Orthodox Church in Nashville, Tennessee

"Evangelism is all about relationships and this book gives us valuable insights into how others find their encounters with us and how we can better make the initial relationship a positive one for Christ's sake."
Father Chad Hatfield, Chancellor of St. Vladimir's Seminary, New York

"This is a helpful collection of ideas that are proven and effective. Thank you Adam for all of this work."
His Grace Bishop JOHN
Auxiliary - Diocese of Worcester and New England

TABLE OF CONTENTS

Forward by Bishop JOHN
Overseer of The Diocese of Worcester and New England

Introduction

Part 1: Entries 1 to 41

Antidoron
Bible Study
Book Club
Bookstore
Business Cards
Charitable Donations Bin
Choir Practice
Christmas Caroling
Church Blog
Clean Restrooms
Coffee Hour
College Students
Cultural Concert
Daily Services
Faithtree
Greeters, Ushers, Hosts
Holiday Meals
Homilies On Evangelism
Homilies On Forgiveness
Icon Classes
Joyful Feast
Ladies Tea
Landscaping
Liturgical Language
Lotion Bars
Monthly Open House
Newspaper Columns
Non-Service Programming

Old Members
Pray For The Children Of Your Church
Prayer Ropes
Press Releases
Questions
Regular Office Hours
Social Media
Super Bowl Party
Support Groups
Teen Activities
Visitor's Bulletin
Volume And Enunciation
Welcome Letters

Part 2: Entries 42 to 69

5K
Acolyte Training/Captains
Al-Anon
Becoming Truly Human
Blood Drive
Christmas Food Boxes
Church Memorabilia
County Fair
Family Movie Night
Family Night
Good Works
Guaranteed Visitors
Home Groups
Lending Library
Military Support
Monastic Connection
Nursing Home
Oblate Program
Paid Youth Director
Pregnancy Clinics
Public Prayer
St. Joseph's Guild
St. Hawaweeny Party
St. Nicholas Party
Specific Internal Fundraising
Vacation Bible/Church School

Way Series
Website

Part 3: Entries 70 to 95

12 Baskets
Antiphonal Chanting/Singing
Climacus Conference
Consignment Sale
ESL Tutoring
Festivals
GED Program
Guest Speakers
Homeschool Co-op
Mission Minded
Movie & Discussion Panel
On-Site Ministry
Outreach Brainstorming
Parish Council Reorientation
Presentations From Organizations
Prison Ministry
Scouting Groups
Service Books
Signage
Spiritual Gifts
Sunday School
Tithe
Tourist/Travel Resources
TV Show
Weekday Childcare
Weekend Seminar

Part 4: Entries 96 to 100

Deacons, Sub-deacons, and Readers
Health & Wellness Services
Orthodox Natural Church Development
Staff Therapist
Start A Mission

Appendix A: Antidoron
Appendix B: Christmas Caroling
Appendix C: Clean Restrooms
Appendix D: College Students
Appendix E: Homilies On Evangelism
Appendix F: Homilies On Forgiveness
Appendix G: Liturgical Language
Appendix H: Acolyte Training/Captains
Appendix I: Becoming Truly Human
Appendix J: Lending Library
Appendix K: Prison Ministry
Appendix L: Orthodox Natural Church Development
Appendix M: Brochures
Appendix N: International Dinner and Fundraiser
Appendix O: Guest Speaker

Forward

We Orthodox in America want unity so that our voices can be heard and so that we can influence our society. This is not an unreasonable desire. Orthodoxy is the faith that Christ established and we must offer Christ's truth to the world. But if we really want to be united and witness appropriately, we need to open our doors and hearts to the world around us. This is particularly true of the un-churched Orthodox, un-churched Christians and the "Nones". Without opening our doors and hearts to these groups, and I dare add recognize our true identity as the Orthodox Church, we will not be taken seriously.

By un-churched Orthodox I mean those Orthodox Christians in America who were baptized but today belong to no parish and are not on any parish roles. I estimate this group to at least 50% of the baptized Orthodox Christians in America. When I did my Clinical Pastoral Education, 65% of the people admitted to the University of Pittsburgh Hospitals who checked off Orthodox Christian on the admissions form wrote none on the line for home parish. There are more baptized Orthodox Christians who are not on our roles than there are who are registered! This was for me an astonishing discovery. The second group we need to pay attention to is that of our un-churched Christian neighbors as well as the quickly growing group called "Nones" (people claiming they are spiritual but don't identify with any religious group). Some of these folks recognize a need in their lives for God but have not found a satisfactory way of meeting it.

Of course we also need to pay attention to those family members of the founders of our parishes who have stopped coming to church. There may be different reasons for their disinterest or absenting themselves from the Church. Many have chosen to give their energies to secular pursuits including sporting and educational activities, while others simply stay home. If church is not their priority, we need to show them why they should change their minds. We need to be the Church Christ established for all nations, a community of love and fellowship. We need to be members of the body of Christ which praises God the Father and takes care of His people and creation. We need to be more than an ethnic group, although we can be a church that makes room for all of the ethnic traditions to prosper. Those who have left the Church need to see us differently before they can justify to themselves why they should come back. They need to discover us as the Church Christ established, not just the Church grandfather built or brought to America with him.

In an attempt to assimilate into American culture, many have chosen to shed ethnic customs. Some believe they have outgrown the customs of their forebears. I believe there can be room in the Church for both groups. Making room would happen when priority is clearly set on the faith. Within the faith, love and tolerance of all cultures will be grown out of real Christian love. If we love one another and we embrace the common faith, we can speak many languages, wear different clothes and dance different dances, even sometimes to the same music. A Church that is chosen by Americans seeking Christ will be more appealing to those former members who are seeking American assimilation. Paradoxically, I believe it will be former Protestant and Roman Catholic Orthodox who will bring our lost Orthodox home.

Our parishes need to open their doors and hearts. Opening doors and hearts are actions or practices. By doing the outreach activities included in this anthology, we can show that our doors and hearts are open. With open hearts and doors, we can then achieve the kind of Orthodox unity that America can be taken seriously.

Bishop JOHN
Diocese of Worcester and New England

Introduction

This book is an attempt to help us see our parishes through the eyes of visitors. I have visited almost 100 Orthodox Churches during my full-time position with the Antiochian Archdiocese of North America. My first impressions range from wonderful to frustrating. I have a deacon at my church who describes his first visit to an Orthodox Church as being half drawn and half repulsed. Are we prepared for the repulsed feelings of a first time visitor who was raised in an anti-Catholic household? Are we pouncing on people with too much enthusiasm and irrelevant information when they show a slight amount of interest in our faith? After 20 years I finally understood Edison's statement about inventing the lightbulb. He found a thousand ways that it did not work. The same could be said for my evangelism efforts. I found a thousand ways to mess up the opportunity. It was not until I understood the entry on questions, entry 33, that the remaining entries began to make sense.

The book is directed towards the entire congregation, both clergy and laity. To put it another way, I do not support clericalism or anti-clericalism. I assume the pastor is the shepherd of the sheep, and sheep beget sheep. Under the pastor's leadership the entire church congregation should be involved in the Great Commission at some level, which is why the church has it read at every baptism.

There are three problems you will encounter when growing your church which are related to this book. The first one relates to visitors you are already receiving. Many will visit your church and not come back. The truth is not always pleasant, and what you think is beautiful might be offensive to a guest. For example some people are angered by the comment that God loves them.

Another problem is keeping your intentions in check while pursuing growth. It can be more difficult than we realize to speak the truth in love. I do not encourage growth for the sake of growth, or growth because your church has financials problems and needs more members to help pay the bills. This book is an expression of the Great Commission according to the Great Commandment. The Great Commission given to us by Jesus is to "Go therefore and make disciples of all nations, baptizing them in the name of the Father and of the Son and of the Holy Spirit, and teaching them to obey everything that I have commanded you" (Matthew 28:19-20). However, we cannot disregard the Great Commandment, "you shall love the Lord your God with all your heart, and with all your soul, and with all your mind, and with all your strength.' The second is this, 'You shall love your neighbor as yourself.' There is no other commandment greater than these" (Mark 12:30-31). Paul said it perfectly when he said that we must be "speaking the truth in love" (Ephesians4:15). How we evangelize matters as much as evangelizing.

The last problem is the one that everyone thinks is the biggest problem. How do we get people to visit? I promise this is the least of your problems. Truly successful ventures are contagious because of the nature of their business. If you focus on the nature of your business, being a joyful Christian community focused on bringing the truth in love to those near you, then the nature of your business will become contagious. Contagious does not mean every visitor will want to join. Contagious means you are doing the best job you can with the visitors you receive at your church.

There are entries in this book which are indirectly related to physical growth but will produce physical growth if you keep your intentions in check. The best expression I have heard to describe this is, "a great commitment to the great commandment according to the great commission produces a great church." Although he is not Orthodox, I believe Rick Warren was spot on with that statement. He took it so seriously that several years ago his ministry team decided to plant a church in every nation around the world to fulfill the Great Commission. They succeeded. How many of us have this same commitment in the Orthodox Church?

The basics of the Orthodox way of life are not included in this book, because they are the first priorities of every pastor for his flock. Regular church attendance, regular participation in the sacraments, prayer, and fasting are all assumed to be top priorities. Also, I assume awareness and understanding that physical growth of a church should always happens with and as a part of spiritual growth. God is infinite, therefore we will always be pursuing God.

I recommend reading this book according to the topics you are most interested in. Do not feel that you have to read the entries according to the order in which they are arranged. Each entry was written independent of the other entries. Each entry is something which has been done and is producing results. Some entries are unique to specific churches, so I have included contact information for that parish. Other entries are a combination of information from multiple parishes such as the entry "Greeters, Ushers, and Hosts."

The entries are organized first according to length of time for implementation and then alphabetically within that time frame. Entries 1-41 are estimated as taking 1-3 months to implement. From 42 to 69 the entries will take approximately 3-6 months to implement. Then entries 70-95 are expected to take about 6-12 months. The last few, items 96-100, could take anywhere from 1-5 years to implement. You will also see any anticipated implementation/ongoing cost estimate included and the minimum number of volunteers needed. This categorical/estimated information is an educated guess, not a guarantee.

In the appendix you will find various articles, documents, and content which supplement certain entries. For example entry #1 is about antidoron. A sample recipe is included as appendix A. For entries which have a corresponding appendix supplement, the letter of the appendix is supplied at the end of the entry.

Lastly I would like to say thank you for reading this book. This means you probably agree with the Very Reverend Fr. Chad Hatfield, Chancellor (CEO) of St. Vladimir's Seminary, when he said:

> There are a lot of people in this country (Christians) who have missiology but no ecclesiology. In other words they love the Lord. They have the Lord, but there is no connection to church. Well we also face in Orthodoxy people that have an ecclesiology but no missiology. So it's not one or the other. We have to recover both, put the pieces together and use every resource we have for building up the body of Christ in this land.

I agree with Fr. Chad that one of the most common problems we face is a disconnect with missiology. I hope this book helps people reconnect with our rich heritage of missiology.

Adam Lowell Roberts

Part 1

1-3 Months

To the best of my knowledge entries 1-41 are the easiest and fastest to implement.

Entry #1

Antidoron

The word means "instead of the gifts" and was originally intended for guests who were not partaking of the Eucharist. This entry is directly related to the entry on Greeters, Ushers, and Hosts. Hosts can take the visitors up (if the visitors desire it) for a blessing from the priest and Holy Bread. The lay helper can also offer to bring back Holy Bread for the visitor, because the visitor may feel uncomfortable during the first visit to approach for a blessing. We need to remember that the bread is blessed and ought to be treated with respect. Make sure the guests know that it should be completely consumed, including crumbs, without dropping any pieces on the floor or throwing away leftover pieces. Also people need training on how to make the Holy Bread. Many churches, including mine, have an instruction book for the bakers. This helps make sure, but obviously cannot guarantee, that the people who have volunteered to bake the bread are following the rubrics of the church on Holy Bread. I have included sample instructions and recipe as appendix A.

- Time Required For Implementation: 1-3 months
- Implementation Cost: $0
- Ongoing Cost: $0
- Required Volunteers: 1

Entry #2

Bible Study

Some people join the Orthodox church and stop reading their Bible. Some people grow up in the Orthodox Church and then later in life pick up their Bible. Some people wonder why other people talk about the Bible. I think you can see where I am going with this. Fr. Alexander Schmemann, in his book *The Eucharist*, referred to the scriptures as "the chief, incomparable and truly *saving* source of faith and life." (Schmemann p.75) Bible studies help re-catechize our existing laity and give a comfortable place for visitors to get to know us. Fr. Gregory Hohnholt at Holy Trinity Greek Orthodox Church in Nashville, TN does a weekly Bible study. One of the regular visitors said they average 20 participants a week. This is also an easy event to invite friends, family, and co-workers to who are not ready or willing to visit a service. Visiting on a Sunday morning is a big deal, and sometimes we forget the stress related. A weekday Bible study removes this stress and gives a soft introduction of your church. If you are looking for curriculum, then look at the New Testament commentary series by Fr. Lawrence Farley available from Ancient Faith Publishing.

- Time Required For Implementation: 1-3 months
- Implementation Cost: $0
- Ongoing Cost: $0
- Required Volunteers: 2

Entry #3

Book Club

Gail Hyatt, wife of Dn. Michael Hyatt at my home parish in Franklin, Tennessee, hosts a book club in her home. Several people from this book club have visited and joined our church. Most of the books are Orthodox, but she has considered others such as *Mere Christianity* by C.S. Lewis. The book club is not taught by Gail. Instead she leads a true discussion about the material. Some of the books they have covered so far include: *Beginning To Pray* by Anthony Bloom, *Our Thoughts Determine Our Lives: The Life and Teachings Of Elder Thaddeus of Vitovnica*, *Gospel of John* by Fr. Lawrence Farley, *Christ In The Psalms* by Patrick Henry Reardon, and *His Life Is Mine* by Archimandrite Sophrony. Gail tries to find books which will include everyone. Also consider alternating back and forth between old and new books.

- Time Required For Implementation: 1-3 months
- Implementation Cost: $0
- Ongoing Cost: $0
- Required Volunteers: 1

Entry #4

Bookstore

Every church I have visited has a bookstore, but hardly any of them are organized. Consider organizing the bookstore according to reader's interest, just like your public library. You should have a section for visitors, one for enquirer's, another for catechumens, and yet one more for members. For visitor's and enquirer's, consider having books like *Coming Home* edited by Fr. Peter Gillquist or *Welcome To The Orthodox Church* by Kh. Frederica Mathewes-Green. The above two book are available online for sale. Depending on the amount of books you have you could categorize even further for the members such as marriage and family. Having at least the four categories mentioned above helps those new to Orthodoxy focus on books which are closer in relevancy to their current level exposure to the Church, instead of visitors accidentally picking up a book intended for existing Orthodox.

- Time Required For Implementation: 1-3 months
- Implementation Cost: $10-50 for signs of categories
- Ongoing Cost: should create profit
- Required Volunteers: 1

Entry #5

Business Cards

Create and freely distribute generic business cards about your parish. I have seen this done by many parishes. Put useful information on the business card. Some pastors use their own business cards because the name of the priest should already be on the card. Include service times, website, office phone and email on the card. On the other side consider putting an icon relevant to the name of your church. Freely distributing business cards can create awareness about the presence of your church. Always have 500-1000 available for the congregation to distribute. Fr. Raphael Barberg at Saint James The Apostle Mission in Westminster, Maryland keeps business cards out for the laity by all of the other literature. He also mentions the business cards at the end of liturgy to guests and encourages them to take one. Handing out business cards is a unique and interesting way to share your church. People will notice a professionalism they might not have encountered with other churches. Please have the business cards professionally designed and printed.

- Time Required For Implementation: 1-3 months
- Implementation Cost: $100 per batch of cards
- Ongoing Cost: $100 per additional order
- Required Volunteers: 1

Entry #6

Charitable Donations Bin

There are many forms of this, but having a charitable donations bin might be one of the easiest forms of ministry. The bins are usually managed by the organization who dropped it off. There are bins for old cell phones, eye glasses, clothes, and more. If you are having a hard time finding a charitable bin to have at your church visit http://www.donationtown.org. Make sure you have someone from the organization do a presentation on how the items are used and who they benefit. If the charitable items are being distributed locally, then try and volunteer to help distribute the items.

- Time Required For Implementation: 1-3 months
- Implementation Cost: $0
- Ongoing Cost: $0
- Required Volunteers: 1

Entry #7

Choir Practice

The idiom "practice makes perfect" might have come from the Orthodox Church, because people can tell when a parish is not practicing its music. If the singing is making it difficult for visitors to enjoy the service, then we are encouraging them to join someone else's church. This is a touchy subject, but there is a difference between a choir who practices and one who does not. I am not talking about the quality of their voices. I have heard mediocre choirs who were prepared have a stronger impact on the worship than other choirs with better singers but less preparation. I would even propose paying a stipend to choir directors who are doing an excellent job. Choir directors, just like anyone else in Church leadership, are talked about behind their back, questioned, and receive many side-ways, eyebrows up stares when the choir gets off key. A good choir director is working hard and deserves a thank you in the form of a stipend. Practice does not have to be every week, although some churches do. Many are scheduling practice either every other week or once a month. Please note the time required for implementation on this entry is exactly that. It is not an estimation for how long it will take for a choir to sound better.

- Time Required For Implementation: 1-3 months
- Implementation Cost: $0
- Ongoing Cost: $0
- Required Volunteers: 5-10

Entry #8

Christmas Caroling

Caroling is not just for protestants, because nothing truly Orthodox will be lost forever. Christmas Caroling can be traced as early as the second century. We sing specific hymns during the nativity fast preparing the coming incarnation. Also, there are many songs we are familiar with which theologically fit into Orthodoxy, such as "Joy To The World" or "O Holy Night." The churches I have seen caroling mix Orthodox hymns in with other carols. This gives people a taste of Orthodoxy without forcing it on them. Locations are not limited to homes. Nursing homes and hospitals are usually grateful for every group of carolers willing to walk the halls. The holidays in a medical facility can be depressing, so even if another group is caroling one week it can be just as exciting for another group to come the next week. Make sure you are not singing songs which are blatantly un-Orthodox, such as "Mary Did You Know?" Yes, she knew! It is called the Feast of the Annunciation! For a suggested list of Christmas carols, see appendix B.

- Time Required For Implementation: 1-3 months
- Implementation Cost: $0
- Ongoing Cost: $0
- Required Volunteers: 4

Entry #9

Church Blog

A church blog is even easier to maintain than a personal blog. If you are looking for content all you have to do is post a story on the saint of the day and how it relates to our lives today. The fastest growing websites have a daily blog, but even a consistent weekly blog will attract online traffic. If you are not blogging daily, make sure blogs are being posted with regularity, such as every Wednesday or every Tuesday and Thursday. If the posts are sporadic they do not attract as much traffic. For more on this visit www.michaelhyatt.com, who is a deacon within the Orthodox Church. With over 500,000 blog followers, he was named by Forbes Magazine as the one person to follow on social media in 2014. He knows blogs.

- Time Required For Implementation: 1-3 months
- Implementation Cost: $40 setup on wordpress.com
- Ongoing Cost: $20 per year for a domain
- Required Volunteers: 1

Entry #10

Clean Restrooms

A protestant study done in recent years listed unclean restrooms as the number one reason a family would not return for repeat visits to a church. Do not think your parish is exempt. All it takes is one bad experience for a mother to yank her family out of there. Not only that, be sure she will tell her friends and families about the unclean restrooms. Restrooms should be well stocked with toilet paper, soap, paper towels or hand driers. Have designated lay volunteers check on the restrooms before, during, and after services. Quality restaurants are religious about clean restrooms. For example J. Alexander's restaurant does a restroom check every 15 minutes during dining hours. How often are your restrooms getting checked? To make it easier on your volunteers create a checklist for them which includes: toilets, toilet paper, floors clean, counters dry, soap, paper towels, trash cans, mirrors. Some restrooms have additional items such as a diaper changing area. Make sure your checklist is relevant to your restroom. A women's restroom checklist should mention feminine care, while the men's might check the floor under the urinals. For an interesting article on first impressions to a church please read this article: www.thomrainer.com/2012/06/30/what_they_see_when_they_come_to_your_church. For a sample restroom checklist see appendix C.

- Time Required For Implementation: 1-3 months
- Implementation Cost: $100 cleaning supplies
- Ongoing Cost: $50 monthly
- Required Volunteers: 1

Entry #11

Coffee Hour

I used to hate coffee hour. Finally I was blessed to hear a podcast episode by Kevin Allen on Ancient Faith Radio about hospitality. Fr. James Kordaris explained how coffee hour is an extension of the Divine Liturgy. It is that first moment after the Eucharist in which we intentionally and yet casually demonstrate that we are a community. With children running, parish council members discussing business, and old friends trying to catch up, coffee hour can be a war zone for visitors. However if we practice the spirit of hospitality then coffee hour changes. It is still stressful when those assigned for setup and cleanup do not show, or a child spills a drink, but when the whole event is handled in the spirit of hospitality the visitors notice the difference. Also make sure to have great coffee at coffee hour, not the cheapest you can find. I am not saying to have Starbucks, but Americans take their coffee seriously. Maybe even different types depending on the size of your parish: bold, mild, featured flavor of the week, etc. Great coffee guarantees that your guests know that you enjoy providing this coffee to them, instead of making them feel like it was an obligation you were not able to get out of. Remember that our goal is to create an environment of hospitality to our guests who are not Orthodox.

- Time Required For Implementation: 1-3 months
- Implementation Cost: $50
- Ongoing Cost: $.50 per cup of coffee including cream and sugar
- Required Volunteers: 2

Entry #12

College Students

Christian churches of all denominations, lose 60-80% of their college students. These numbers are also true in the Orthodox Church. There are two options to encourage which can and are reducing these numbers in the Orthodox Church. The first help is in the form of OCF (Orthodox Christian Fellowship). If your parish is near a college campus make sure there is an active OCF chapter. If there is one then try to help it out. If there is not one then it needs to be started. OCF keeps the Orthodox students connected throughout the school year. As of 2015 only 5% of college campuses have an OCF chapter. During the summer encourage the students to get involved with an Orthodox summer camp. In 2014 I interviewed many of the staff at an Orthodox camp in South Carolina. They all said being at camp made a difference in their spiritual life. Camp helped them see how important God was. Appendix D has a list of Orthodox camping programs in North America. The last thing is to make sure college students who are visiting your parish are invited to holiday meals.

- Time Required For Implementation: 1-3 months
- Implementation Cost: $0
- Ongoing Cost: $0
- Required Volunteers: 1

Entry #13

Cultural Concert

Many churches have a strong ethnic membership. This ethnic membership can be used to put on concerts for the public featuring your cultural music, musicians, and singers. St. Mary's Orthodox Cathedral in Minneapolis has had a Balalaika Orchestra since 1954. The orchestra currently has 15 members and features slavic music from Russia and various parts of Europe. You church may only have one musician/artist, and that can be just as entertaining as a full group. For more information about St. Mary's Orchestra or how to book them visit www.stmarysoca.org/balalaika.html.

- Time Required For Implementation: 1-3 months
- Implementation Cost: $0
- Ongoing Cost: should create profit
- Required Volunteers: 2

Entry #14

Daily Services

Daily services are not just for monasteries. It only takes one dedicated person to establish daily services. As the word is spread, more and more will attend. You may only average two to three people during the week, but is that really a valid argument against daily services? If the pastor is part-time or works a full-time job, consider the value of readers services. Dn. Andrew Bardwell in Homer, Alaska has been conducting readers services at All Saints Orthodox Church for two years since their priest was transferred. While not daily, he does a Wednesday Orthros and Vespers, Saturday Vespers, Sunday morning Typika, and Vespers on a Feast Day. Even without a priest he is having more services a week than most parishes I visit. Daily services can be a great evangelism tool for those heavily involved in other faiths. Five pastors of other Christian denominations have joined St. John's Cathedral in Eagle River, Alaska because of weekly services. Those were the only services they were able to attend, because they worked full-time at their own church.

- Time Required For Implementation: 1-3 months
- Implementation Cost: $0
- Ongoing Cost: $0
- Required Volunteers: 1

Entry #15

Faithtree

St. Michael's Orthodox Church in Van Nuys, California runs a program called *Faithtree*. The program was started by Michelle Moujaes, a lay person! *Faithtree* was started by Michelle because she wanted to help her parish be Orthodox seven days a week. Orthodoxy is a way of life, and *Faithtree* helps the people at St. Michael's connect with that way. *Faithtree* is in charge of scheduling guest speakers, workshops, small groups, and online learning opportunities. All of these events are opportunities to invite a guest. The website is professional, extensive, and has lots to offer. You can learn more at www.faithtree.org.

- Time Required For Implementation: 1-3 months
- Implementation Cost: $0
- Ongoing Cost: $0
- Required Volunteers: 1

Entry #16

Greeters, Ushers, and Hosts

I wish I was the only person who could say they have visited a church without a single person ever saying a word to them. Your greeters should be the friendliest people in your church, the ones who have never met a stranger and are best friends with strangers within minutes. They make introverts feel calm and extroverts excited. They pull the visitors information such as name and where they are from so casually the visitor doesn't even notice. The OCA has a presentation which states visitors do not want to be called out by name during or after the service. Whether you publicly announce your visitors or not, getting their name and address is valuable (read more Entry #41 Welcome Letter). Try to have at least two greeters. If you don't, Murphy's Law will produce two different guests at the same time. Next, the Greeter should be prepared to hand off the visitors to an Usher. The Usher should be pre share literature or bulletins with the guest. Fr. Constantine Nasr in Oklahoma City recommends having DVDs available to give guests. Several videos are available on YouTube for download to a DVD. *Journey To Antioch* shows the journey of the former EOC church into the Antiochian Orthodox Church of North America. *Have A Little Faith* by Soul Pancake has the host, Zach Anner, visiting St. Sophia's Greek Orthodox Cathedral in Los Angeles to "learn more about his grandma's church." Also, there are a series of introductory videos on Orthodoxy available at www.goarch.org in the video section of the multimedia programs link. The Ushers will then guide the guests to a host who will sit with the guests during the service and invite them to coffee hour after the Liturgy. Once a guest knows someone they are more likely to attend coffee hour and open up about why they are visiting.

- Time Required For Implementation: 1-3 months
- Implementation Cost: $50 for name tags
- Ongoing Cost: $0
- Required Volunteers: 2

Entry #17

Holiday Meals

Many people are alone during the holidays. Some families may be willing to have a certain number of guests join them for a holiday meal. Other parishioners are single and have organized larger meals together. A few churches are known for allowing parishioners to use the parish hall and kitchen because a large group wants to come together for a holiday meal but no one has enough space. Encourage parishioners to bring a friend to these holiday meals. Putting emphasis and intention into holidays meals helps your congregation experience the Orthodox family.

- Time Required For Implementation: 1-3 months
- Implementation Cost: $0
- Ongoing Cost: $0
- Required Volunteers: 2

Entry #18

Homilies On Evangelism

Regular homilies on the Orthodox approach to evangelism are important and available. In my opinion every gospel reading throughout the year has an evangelistic aspect. The more evangelism is talked about the more parishioners will remember how important it is. Fr. Chad Hatfield, Chancellor (CEO) of St. Vladimir's Theological Orthodox Seminary, says it this way, "ecclesilogy requires missiology, and missiology requires ecclesiology." Also, a multi-Sunday series of homilies on evangelism can be effective. Fr. Andrew Stephen Damick in Emmaus, Pennsylvania did a 10 part series on evangelism. This put evangelism in the face of the regular visitors and those who come sparingly. Visit www.saintpaulemmaus.org for more information on that series. The script of Fr. Andrew's first homily and a link to the podcast version is available in appendix E.

- Time Required For Implementation: 1-3 months
- Implementation Cost: $0
- Ongoing Cost: $0
- Required Volunteers: 1

Entry #19

Homilies On Forgiveness

Homilies On Forgiveness: Every business owner knows that a large part of growing a business is not losing the customers you have. This principle also applies to our churches. Dn. Michael Hyatt said during one of his podcast episodes of "The Intersection of East and West" that you are more likely to be offended at church than anywhere else. If we flip that around it also means you are also more likely to offend. Schisms usually happen from people being offended by something. Forgiveness is often misunderstood in America, even by those in our own parishes! There is much literature about forgiveness in Orthodoxy, but one of my favorite quotes comes from the motivational speaker Andy Andrews when he said, "forgiveness is about the past, trust is about the future." The Antiochian Archdiocese has a program on forgiveness and reconciliation available from the Department of Lay Ministry. I have included some sample material on forgiveness from my blog in appendix F.

- Time Required For Implementation: 1-3 months
- Implementation Cost: $0
- Ongoing Cost: $0
- Required Volunteers: 1

Entry #20

Icon Classes

Have people bring in icons from home to the church and a priest/someone educated can explain the theology of the icons. This explanation of the icon could even serve as the homily. Then the people in the parish who own that icon have a story to share with guests who visit their home. Also keep plenty of diptychs and triptychs in the bookstore. Many non-Orthodox find these interesting and would appreciate them as gifts. Fr. Peter Gillquist, of blessed memory, often told a story of a lady who was considering becoming Orthodox but was struggling with the Theotokos. Fr. Peter gave her an icon of the Theotokos and asked her to keep the icon around while she prayed. Within one week the woman said she was now fine with the Theotokos and had become a part of her life.

- Time Required For Implementation: 1-3 months
- Implementation Cost: $0
- Ongoing Cost: $0
- Required Volunteers: 1

Entry #21

Joyful Feast

We have many times throughout the year when we celebrate breaking the fast. Whether Nativity, Dormition, or Pascha, a public joyful feast focused on the celebration of God is a great opportunity to invite friends and family. My particular favorite is Agape Vespers if your parish focuses more on a Christian celebration instead of an excuse for other things. We should be celebrating the feast of the Church. If your feast is an expression of a joyful Christian community then consider inviting your friends and family. To be clear, I am not suggesting you invite them to the service. For example, I used to invite people to the Pascha service thinking they would appreciate the joy of that service. Not a single person has ever been willing to return for another visit. What I now focus on instead is Agape Vespers. The service is short and less threatening yet retains the joy of the resurrection. In some churches it might even make sense to invite people to just the meal after Agape Vespers. The goal here is to expose the community to your joyful Christian community, so be open minded when considering this option.

- Time Required For Implementation: 1-3 months
- Implementation Cost: $0 if you accept donations or schedule a potluck
- Ongoing Cost: $0
- Required Volunteers: 1

Entry #22

Ladies Tea

Every year around Ascension the ladies of St. Andrew Orthodox Church in Riverside, California host a tea for ladies and young girls of the church. "Ladies bring tasty delicacies and finger foods to share and a wide array of delightful teas are served... It is a popular occasion to invite non-Orthodox family and friends to the parish." Some churches hold the tea on Bright Saturday immediately after the Feast of the Mother of God of the "Life-Giving Spring." For a change of pace some churches will rotate homes to host the tea instead of always having it at the church, which can be an easier environment for some people to invite non-Orthodox friends and family. For more information about St. Andrew's tea visit www.saintandrew.net/antiochianwomen.html.

- Time Required For Implementation: 1-3 months
- Implementation Cost: $0
- Ongoing Cost: $0 if potluck style
- Required Volunteers: 1

Entry #23

Landscaping

The quality of your landscaping gives the first impression to visitors before they meet anyone. Is the grass mowed? Are there flowers? When were the flower/mulch beds last cleaned and weeded? For those without landscaping experts in the parish, focus on simple solutions and visit your local nursery. Nurseries will give you free advice on landscaping when you buy their plants. Focus on smaller, local nurseries for plants, because they will do a better job at stocking plants which are naturally from your region. Big box stores sometimes stock beautiful plants which will not survive your region after one year. Landscaping can also be a part of your homeschooling co-op if you have enough teenagers. They can learn real landscaping skills which can then be used as job skills later on. Some churches will even change the colors of the flowers outside to match the liturgical colors inside.

- Time Required For Implementation: 1-3 months
- Implementation Cost: $500-1,500
- Ongoing Cost: depends on amount of landscaping
- Required Volunteers: 4

Entry #24

Liturgical Language

The liturgy has always been in the language of the people. St. Cyril and Methodius translated the Greek services into Slavonic, so that the Russian people could worship in their own language. We cannot forget the commandment given to us at every baptism, the great commission. How can we say we are preaching the gospel when it is in a language the local community does not understand. I am not saying that all services in America should be in English. I am saying exactly this: it should be in the language of the community. Please keep in mind this is a process of trial and error. If your church is embedded in a Hispanic community and there is no Spanish in your service, then you should reconsider your service. If your parish contains 90% Greeks, Arabs, Russians, or Ukrainians, then it makes sense when your services are in those languages. I understand having parts of a service in other languages. This is a great ministry to those in the parish who speak that language. Some Orthodox churches will proclaim the Lord's Prayer and the Nicene Creed in several languages. This too is beautiful. All it takes is some minor researching of Orthodox history to see we have always had the liturgy in the language of the people, not the language we were told was the right way of having the liturgy. An excellent article was written on the topic of English services by Robert Arakaki titled, "Why Americans Need An All-English Liturgy." This article first appeared on orthodoxbridge.com. I have included a copy of the article as appendix G. Also the homily should be preached in the language which will be understood by the majority of the people. For example, if the church is predominantly Arabic speaking, then a homily in Arabic makes the most sense. For those who do not speak Arabic an English translation could be printed in the bulletin.

- Time Required For Implementation: 1-3 months
- Implementation Cost: $0
- Ongoing Cost: $0
- Required Volunteers: 1

Entry #25

Lotion Bars

In Iowa City, Iowa at St. Raphael of Brooklyn Orthodox Church the congregations is putting good use to the left over beeswax candle fragments. Through a series of trial and error they were able to development 2 ounce lotion bars. The lotion looks like a bar of soap but "softens in contact with skin." Current ingredients include: sweet almond oil, recycled pure beeswax, organic shea butter, organic cocoa butter, kokum butter, and vitamin E oil. All of this comes in a nice little oval-shaped metal container. The bars can be sold at flea markets, county fairs, local farmers market, and at church. For information email eglotionbar@gmail.com or call the church at 319-337-6784. Please note that it is inappropriate to use blessed candles in this way.

- Time Required For Implementation: 1-3 months
- Implementation Cost: $50-100
- Ongoing Cost: should create profit
- Required Volunteers: 1

Entry #26

Monthly Open House

In Upper Darby, PA Fr. Joel Gillam hosts a monthly open house after the first Saturday in each month with Vespers. The service is calm, peaceful, short, and the least threatening. This open-house is a dedicated time when parishioners know they can bring people to an event for visitors. The open house includes coffee and pastries, a short presentation on Orthodoxy, and Q&A time. Fr. Joel says if you are trying to decide when to have the open house, choose an evening which gives the priest the most time to spend with the visitors. A monthly intentional event prepared for visitors (not on a Sunday morning) creates an easier opportunity for people to visit. Having the open house during the evening makes it easier to attend because it does not disrupt their current Sunday morning commitments.

- Time Required For Implementation: 1-3 months
- Implementation Cost: $100 welcome packets and refreshments
- Ongoing Cost: $50 per month
- Required Volunteers: 2

Entry #27

Newspaper Columns

At Holy Cross Orthodox Church in Daytona Beach, Florida Fr. Michael Byars has been having articles on Orthodoxy published in the local newspaper for years. He said it helps to have a religious editor or a religious section. There are several positive effects from this effort. First, Fr. Michael is able to preach the gospel to those who may not know about the Orthodox faith or may be homebound. Also, Fr. Michael is able to announce upcoming events which may be initially more interesting to the public such as a festival. Also, Fr. Michael is able to connect with the community when they see an Orthodox article in their local paper. Holy Cross is shown as part of their community. This newspaper article also gives Fr. Michael the opportunity to offer the Orthodox perspective to his local community on current events.

- Time Required For Implementation: 1-3 months
- Implementation Cost: $0
- Ongoing Cost: $0
- Required Volunteers: 1

Entry #28

Non-Service Programming

For most of his 33 years when he was a parish priest Bishop John Abdalah, who oversees the Diocese of Worcester and New England, was either taking a class or teaching a class. Continuing education is a critical component of the Orthodox way. Consider holding at least two different kinds of weekly non-service programming in addition to services (not instead of). If you do not have any additional programming in place start with only one. You can work up to a second program over time. For many churches the easiest thing to do is have a running enquirer's class. Allow yourself three to six months to schedule, prepare, and successfully launch a teaching class. Ongoing adult education is important. We should never stop learning. There is a reason so many saints have been known to give long homilies, because we needed the education. This need has not subsided. Also consider having the program at different times. For some communities having the program during the day on a weekday is easier. A good resource for pastors is the *Resource Book For Mission And Evangelism* by Fr. Constantine Nasr. The book is available by sending a request to Nasr Orthodox Foundation, 14709 Brasswood Parkway, Edmond, OK 73013. If you want ideas for content see the entry on Bible Studies.

- Time Required For Implementation: 1-3 months
- Implementation Cost: $0
- Ongoing Cost: $0
- Required Volunteers: 2

Entry #29

Old Members

Call less active/inactive members during a slow period of the church calendar (summer, early fall, etc.) and offer a house blessing. Most will accept your offer and may even want you to stay for dinner. Outside of pre-Lent a nice dinner is easier to schedule. Make sure you avoid making them feel guilty for not attending, because that is not the purpose of your phone call. If you genuinely make your purpose a house blessing and the desire to reconnect, then there is a greater chance of achieving that reconnection. Trying to make people feel guilty for not attending church creates division, not reconciliation.

- Time Required For Implementation: 1-3 months
- Implementation Cost: $0
- Ongoing Cost: $5 per household
- Required Volunteers: 1

Entry #30

Pray For The Children Of Your Church

Growth can also come in the form of members of the parish having babies. Praying for the children of your church, who are the future of the parish, is important. Many women in our American Orthodox Churches come together weekly or monthly and pray the Akathist together (some even as a reader's service) and then pray over the children of that parish. They will name every child in that church and pray for him/her.

- Time Required For Implementation: 1-3 months
- Implementation Cost: $0
- Ongoing Cost: $0
- Required Volunteers: 2

Entry #31

Prayer Ropes

I first learned how to make prayer ropes when I was on staff at the Antiochian Village in 1998. I was blessed to learn some important rules concerning prayer ropes, one of which fits here. It is preferred that people give away their prayer ropes instead of keep them. They make wonderful gifts for those in your life who are active/struggling Christians and are not Orthodox. Avoid Orthodox terminology when explaining them and their purpose. Stick to basic, common Christian terminology they can understand and embrace. I frequently tell people they are similar to the "WWJD" bracelets, because the purpose of them is to remind us to talk to God about all things. If you do not have anyone who knows how to make them in your church, then invite a guest to do a workshop. You could also schedule a visit to a monastery to learn how to make them. Another idea mentioned to me was to have a dedicated prayer rope making session before Vespers on Saturdays. For example, for about an hour before Saturday Vespers a group would come together to make prayer ropes together and teach others who are interested. You could even have people take turns reading the psalms or the lives of the saints.

- Time Required For Implementation: 1-3 months
- Implementation Cost: $0
- Ongoing Cost: $0
- Required Volunteers: 1

Entry #32

Press Releases

Send out a press release for all parish events and changes to the local news media. Events and changes can be new iconography, the visit of a bishop, a scheduled presentation, a 10 week series on marriage and family. There are many Orthodox in our communities who have disconnected from the church. Seeing the Orthodox Church in the news is a great way to reconnect with those lost members. Many of your press releases will be ignored, but some will get picked up to be included in the news. Submitting a press release is free, just make sure they are professionally written, formatted, and submitted. Local public relations firms can you help design your template for submissions. Use local PR firms because they will have strong relationships with the local media that national PR firms may not have. Also, local PR firms may know of places to submit press releases that you have not thought of because of the religious nature of Orthodox press releases.

- Time Required For Implementation: 1-3 months
- Implementation Cost: $0
- Ongoing Cost: $0
- Required Volunteers: 1

Entry #33

Questions

During a flight to Miami I was reading *The Orthodox* Church by Timothy Ware. The lady next to me asked within minutes of me pulling it out of my bag, "Are you with the Orthodox Church?" The old me would have gone into a five to ten minute elaborate detailed answer of my job and devotion to the Church. Instead of that, I turned to her and asked, "Oh, how do you know about the Orthodox Church?" And thank God I did! She began telling me about this horrific experience with an ethnic church she had visited. Her co-worker was Orthodox, and the co-worker's family cared more for their ethnic heritage and cultural traditions than the truth of Orthodoxy. After 10 minutes of learning everything I could about her experiences, I finally told her about my job with the Church but it was only after learning as much as I could. Learn how to ask more questions, promote more questions, and stop trying to find the silver bullet answer. St. Innocent had to find out more before he could relate. Paul had to find out more before he could relate. Even God in the Old and New Testament asked questions for our benefit, not for His. Ask more questions. Help your parish focus on being interested, not interesting. Being interested is how you love your neighbor and make disciples in all nations.

- Time Required For Implementation: 1-3 months
- Implementation Cost: $0
- Ongoing Cost: $0
- Required Volunteers: 1

Entry #34

Regular Office Hours

We have many parishes without a full-time pastor, or without a pastor at all. Regular office hours does not mean someone in church leadership being in the office full-time. Regular means regular hours which are posted on the door and on the website. If your church can only have a secretary two days a week for four hours, then post that as the office hours. Regular office hours provide stability for a struggling parish. Knowing someone is there at a particular time, even if it is only on Mondays, can give peace of mind to many parishioners and visitors. Also, pastors live a demanding life with hospital visits, home visits, etc. A church secretary who can reach the pastor makes it easier to keep regular office hours than for the pastor to feel like he is trapped at church from 9-5 Monday through Friday. I have noticed most churches close the office at least one day a week. Make sure to announce and make clear to the congregation which day of the week is the pastor's day off. Of course the pastor is always available for emergencies. However, many people will leave the pastor alone on his day off if they are asked if it can wait until tomorrow. If the office has to be closed, try to post a notice on the door, send out an email to the church, and post a message on the website.

- Time Required For Implementation: 1-3 months
- Implementation Cost: $0
- Ongoing Cost: $0
- Required Volunteers: 1

Entry #35

Social Media

We have to go where the people are to minister to them, just like Jesus having dinner with the sinners, tax collectors, etc. Social Media has more than its fair share of sinners and needs more Orthodox Churches involved. Another way to say this is that Social Media needs our Orthodox presence. There are all sorts of strong feelings about social media and Orthodoxy. Whether you like it or not, it can help you gain visitors to your church and traffic on your website. If you do not know where to start, then start with the two heavyweights: Facebook and Twitter. You need to know that they are different and have different personalities. For Twitter I would read up on Dn. Michael Hyatt, named as the one person to follow on social media in 2014 by Forbes magazine. For Facebook I would suggest researching Amy Porterfield. She is one of the leading strategists for Facebook. There are more and more social media "tribes" showing up every day, and unless you have volunteers in your church who you trust to present a reverent presence of your church on that social media presence, I would focus on the two heavyweights. After Facebook and Twitter, considering having a presence on the following platforms: LinkedIn, Google+, Instagram, and Pinterest. Different regions of the country will gravitate to different social media outlets, so try to discern from your young adults and teens where they are spending their time.

- Time Required For Implementation: 1-3 months
- Implementation Cost: $0
- Ongoing Cost: $0
- Required Volunteers: 1

Entry #36

Super Bowl

The Super Bowl is still one of the largest viewed specials on TV. Organize hosting a party at the parish hall. By setting up a projector and sound system this party can have large appeal at your church to guests. If you do not have easy access to TV channels you can often stream the game online if you have high speed internet access at your church. You may experience a short delay but the quality can be excellent. Make sure your parishioners invite as many people as possible.

- Time Required For Implementation: 1-3 months
- Implementation Cost: $500 snacks and audio/visual equipment
- Ongoing Cost: $0 if potluck or charging for snacks
- Required Volunteers: 2

Entry #37

Support Group

Hosting a support group, such as AA meetings, requires having your own space, and some smaller churches are renting space only on Saturday nights and Sunday mornings. Other than those who do not have a permanent location, every parish should have enough room for a support group. For example, hosting AA meetings is great exposure for your parish. The people coming to those meetings probably value or will soon value community. Due to the "anonymous" nature of AA and other support groups, there may be some in the church who are currently attending a support group and you do not know it. For more information on AA visit www.aa.org. Search the site for the "New Group Form." Fr. Timothy Sas in Duluth, MN runs two versions of AA. He has one traditional version and another Orthodox version. The website for his parish is www.12holyapostles.org. Another formal support group available is SA(sexaholics anonymous). While the idea of this can be offensive to some, SA is a valid support group and has been endorsed by Dr. Albert Rossi, adjunct professor at St. Vladimir's seminary, during one of his podcasts on Ancient Faith Radio. For more information on SA visit www.sa.org. Support is needed in a wide range of areas, so consider this when establishing support groups. Consider grief, parenting, and marriage, and other addictive behaviors such as gambling. If you are using third-party materials for your support group, then make sure their teachings do not conflict in any way with Orthodox dogma.

- Time Required For Implementation: 1-3 months
- Implementation Cost: $0
- Ongoing Cost: utilities and coffee
- Required Volunteers: 1

Entry #38

Teen Activities

Lock-ins are popular at all churches, not just Orthodox. If you want to encourage the teens to invite their non-Orthodox friends, then consider how parents of the non-Orthodox teens will feel about the schedule of events and curriculum if anything will be taught. Consider having two different kinds of lock-ins each year. One could be formatted to help current teens, while the other could be designed as friendly for non-Orthodox friends.

- Time Required For Implementation: 1-3 months
- Implementation Cost: $5-10 per teen for snacks
- Ongoing Cost: same
- Required Volunteers: 1 chaperone per gender

Entry #39

Visitor's Bulletin

For someone's first visit to an Orthodox Church hand out a visitor's bulletin in addition to the regular bulletin for them to read during their first visit. Be ok with the idea of them reading these materials during the service or after. Put information in the bulletin you would want to tell a visitor but may be unable to because the service is going on. This could include additional information about the Divine Liturgy, the Orthodox Church, and your particular parish. You can also invite them to coffee hour after the service in this visitor's bulletin. Also mention Sunday school and nursery times, ages, and locations.

- Time Required For Implementation: 1-3 months
- Implementation Cost: $0
- Ongoing Cost: $1 per bulletin
- Required Volunteers: 1

Entry #40
Volume And Enunciation

Visiting a church with low volume and/or poor enunciation is like visiting one in another language. The ability to worship becomes limited if we cannot hear what is going on. Fortunately this is easier to remedy than services in a different language. The first thing to do is install a microphone system. There are two ways to install a microphone. The first way is to put a lapel microphone on the clergy. This is nicer but more expensive because a good wireless system starts around $500. The easier and cheaper way is to have a stationary microphone in the altar area (never on the altar), and then one on the ambo.

- Time Required For Implementation: 1-3 months
- Implementation Cost: $0-$500
- Ongoing Cost: $0
- Required Volunteers: 1

Entry #41
Welcome Letters

Someone, either greeter, usher, or lay helper, should capture the visitors address or encourage them to fill out a visitors card. St. Philips Orthodox Church in Souderton, PA keeps a visitor's log next to the front doors. Seeing a list of others who have volunteered their name, address, and email helps visitors feel safe about leaving their own private information. On Monday mail out a welcome letter. Please mail this card while the visit is fresh on their mind. Include some information on the Orthodox Church in a soft way, because they probably came with some knowledge of the Orthodox Church. Share contact information, website, and how to contact the pastor if they have questions. Thank them for visiting and tell them you hope they visit again. The highest priority of this letter is to be friendly, not pushy. If there is any pressure or heaviness in the letter they are likely not to visit again. You can also mention important dates coming up they might be interested in, or mention ministries the church is conducting they might have interest in such as Sunday school for children, teen activities, etc. Think of this letter like a thank you card for a wedding gift. There is no pressure, only thanksgiving. If you would like a sample of a visitor card, then please visit this website: www.goarch.org/archdiocese/departments/outreach/visitorcard.

- Time Required For Implementation: 1-3 months
- Implementation Cost: $0
- Ongoing Cost: $1 per visiting household
- Required Volunteers: 1

Part 2

3-6 Months

Entries 42 to 69

Entry #42
5K

Organize a 5K with all of the money donated to a local non-profit organization. 5K races are easy to organize and do not take a lot of volunteers compared to other projects. Typically you will need at least three months to plan and execute but six is ideal. You may need to hire an organizer the first time who is familiar with 5K benefit runs, but if you pay attention you will only need to hire someone one time. Make sure all of the money is publicly donated to a respected charity, not some obscure project within your church. The non-profit will work with you on resources and promotions to help create a large crowd.

- Time Required For Implementation: 3-6 months
- Implementation Cost: $500-1,500
- Ongoing Cost: should break even and donate profits
- Required Volunteers: 5

Entry #43
Acolyte Training/Captains

Acolytes need training. Acolytes affect the fluidity of the service, and visitors will notice if the service is organized or chaotic. We only have one chance to make a first impression, and acolyte behavior will make a large impression on visiting families. Some churches have the same acolytes every Sunday, but some churches have so many they have to rotate. Make sure your acolyte rubrics are clear. At my church I am in charge of 35 acolytes. If we have visiting clergy some of them immediately forget how to serve. Also, our average Sunday servers include four deacons and two priests. Without practice and captains we would struggle. To make things clear I created a sheet of sign language for us to communicate from one side to the other. We also have a second sheet printed and displayed of our practices. The captains are responsible for training the junior acolytes. I stand on the south side and another gentleman stands on the north side. With our presence and guidance we hope to train up clergy, monastics, and at the least a reverence and appreciation for the services. We are about to begin a rotation for Saturday evening Vespers because of growing interest. I have included the sign language and sheet of rubrics we use at my church as appendix H. Contact me if you would like a digital copy.

- Time Required For Implementation: 3-6 months
- Implementation Cost: $0
- Ongoing Cost: $0
- Required Volunteers: 1

Entry #44
Al-Anon

Al-Anon is a support group for family and friends of those with drinking problems. If you are considering having an AA group at your church, then you should consider having Al-Anon as well for the family. The struggle of an alcoholic can often and is usually more damaging on those around the alcoholic. As friends confide in friends, having an Al-Anon group available might be the first place someone seeks help for their loved one if the alcoholic is not seeking help yet. For more information visit www.al-anon.org.

- Time Required For Implementation: 3-6 months
- Implementation Cost: $0
- Ongoing Cost: $0
- Required Volunteers: 1

Entry #45

Becoming Truly Human

The Antiochian Archdiocese began a program in 2013 called "Becoming Truly Human." Once a week for several weeks there is a session which begins with a meal, then moves to a presentation on the basics of Christianity, and finishes with a small group discussion. To fulfill Ephesians 4:11-12, the program is lay lead with the priest as the spiritual advisor. The entire program is gentle, inviting, and easy for non-Christians and the un-Churched to enjoy. I am the current Program Director, implementing this program throughout North America. The program is available to all jurisdictions. For more information visit www.becomingtrulyhuman.com. An article about the program written by Charles Ajalat, Fr. George Kevorkian, Fr. Michael Nasser, and myself is included as appendix I.

- Time Required For Implementation: 3-6 months
- Implementation Cost: $0 for Antiochian churches
- Ongoing Cost: travel costs for on-site training
- Required Volunteers: 6

Entry #46

Blood Drive

The American Red Cross is always looking for locations to hold blood drives. The Red Cross has a strong reputation of good will concerning blood drives. Hosting this on-site will gather lots of attention from within and outside of your church. Many Orthodox Churches are embracing this idea because of the simplicity and obvious value in it. For more information on hosting a blood drive visit www.redcrossblood.org/hosting-blood-drive.

- Time Required For Implementation: 3-6 months
- Implementation Cost: $0
- Ongoing Cost: $0
- Required Volunteers: 2

Entry #47

Christmas Food Boxes

My church delivers boxes of food to a list of families every year on the Saturday before Christmas. We gather the list from a local non-profit called GraceWorks. GraceWorks is known for helping those in need and does a better job of screening the requests for help. In November we tell them how many families we would like to deliver and they give us a list. We are also allowed to leave with the families prayer cards or information on our church. Many of our parishioners stay and pray with the family they have delivered to. Our local grocery store, Publix, even boxes all of the items together for us. All we have to do with Publix is gift them a list of what we want in each box and they volunteer their time to sort the goods. The larger items such as turkeys and milk are left out, but that has been easy for us to administrate.

- Time Required For Implementation: 3-6 months
- Implementation Cost: $0
- Ongoing Cost: $0
- Required Volunteers: 2

Entry #48

Church Memorabilia

Hire a professional graphic designer to have shirts, hats, and other items designed to sell. There are two thoughts behind pricing the items. Some parishes use the bookstore and other saleable items to raise money for the church. I can see the value of this in a bookstore as long as you do not price yourself out of business. For shirts and hats I recommend charging just over cost. This will increase your sales numbers which means more people will be wearing your hats and shirts out in public. If the goal is to spread the word then make the cost as low as possible. For example I have designed an Orthodox bumper sticker. The bumper sticker says, "Orthodoxy: Loving Our Neighbor Since 33 A.D." You are welcome to copy the phrase and print your own instead of ordering from me if that is easier for you.

- Time Required For Implementation: 3-6 months
- Implementation Cost: $100-500
- Ongoing Cost: should create profit
- Required Volunteers: 1

Entry #49

County Fair

Make your booth fun and interesting. Include all the usual items from a bookstore such as icons and prayer ropes. Make sure parishioners manning the booth give good and loving answers when people ask questions. Also, have items to give away to people such as icon cards. Make sure you have a take away with the church's information such as a business card or maybe the most recent bulletin. Stock the booth with literature on the Orthodox Church, the history of your parish in the county, and how your parish is involved in the community. If you have an iconographer in your parish have him/her visit the booth and advertise when he/she will be there, because iconography is foreign to most Americans. Some parishes even sell loaves of bread (unblessed because we do not know what they will do with it) made according the prosphora recipe with short explanations of Holy Bread attached to the loaves. If your parish has some unique ethnicities in your community, then offering their food or cultural items for sale can also make your booth interesting. Some churches will play Orthodox music CDs or Ancient Faith Radio in their booth. If you are looking for more contemporary music consider playing some songs by someone like Kh. Gigi Shadid, who has recorded several CD's of kids music. You can preview and purchase the music here: https://itunes.apple.com/us/artist/gigi-baba-shadid/id484810205. Make sure you get permission from the county fair board for everything you want to do.

- Time Required For Implementation: 3-6 months
- Implementation Cost: $500-2000
- Ongoing Cost: same
- Required Volunteers: 10+

Entry #50

Family Movie Night

Family Movie Night: Many parks throughout America will show a family movie on a large projector. Some parks will do this weekly while others may only do this two or three times during the summer. You can do the same at your church and invite the public. An outside movie night is best but indoors can be good enough if you provide a good screen and sound system. Make sure you have refreshments available for purchase. Also, if you do this indoors then you can do it year round. I recommend making this fun and light. Do not use this event to proselytize people or pressure them into learning more about Orthodoxy. The goal of this event is to provide a safe and loving environment for people to enjoy quality family time. They will naturally be interested in your church because of the event. Consider showing non-Orthodox movies such as *The Wizard of Oz*, *The Sound of Music*, or *A Charlie Brown Christmas*. One of my favorites is the animated *Anastasia* from 1998. It has several references to the Orthodox Church and yet people do not realize it.

- Time Required For Implementation: 3-6 months
- Implementation Cost: $100-500 snacks, audio/visual equipment
- Ongoing Cost: should create profit with donations
- Required Volunteers: 2

Entry #51

Family Night

This is another opportunity to invite friends and family to a low-pressure environment. Fr. Matthew Howell, pastor of St. Herman's Orthodox Church in Wasilla, Alaska, holds family night on Tuesdays. That is when they have Sunday School, adult education, and a reader's Vespers for the parents with babies not old enough for Sunday School. On a side note, Fr. Matthew believes having family night on a non-fasting day has increased attendance because every family night begins with a meal. The non-fasting day has also made it easier finding volunteers to cook. Family night is not just for families, because everyone is invited. The church is a family, and it might be someone's only family. Having a family night which emphasizes community and ongoing education can do wonders for a church.

- Time Required For Implementation: 3-6 months
- Implementation Cost: $0
- Ongoing Cost: $0 (dinners are by donation or potluck)
- Required Volunteers: 3-5

Entry #52

Good Works

Doing organized good works/humanitarian projects helps us stay connected to humility and remember the true reason we do good works, as an expression of thankfulness to God for all He has done. I offer two categories in this entry, anonymous and named. You may think doing anonymous works cannot help your church grow, but the anonymous works inspire a joyful spirit in your parish which becomes contagious to others in the local community. Doing anonymous good works fits into the category of "when you fast hide your face" so that our reward for these good works is in heaven and not here on earth. These good works include anonymous donations or volunteering behind the scenes at a non-profit organization such as cleaning the dishes at a soup kitchen without credit. In the 1990s there was a church putting ads on billboards with loving messages from God in the Bible and they did not put their name or phone number on the billboard. No one ever found out who they were. That is an anonymous good work. In contrast, doing local good works/humanitarian in the name of your parish helps your community to know that your church is having a positive impact. You are not doing this to brag but instead to offer a place for those looking for organizations to connect with who give back to the community. Many people see the church as a country club for the saved, so doing good works in the name of your church shows how important humanitarian projects are to Christians. This can come in the form of sponsorships, donations, volunteer efforts, and more.

- Time Required For Implementation: 3-6 months
- Implementation Cost: $0
- Ongoing Cost: $0
- Required Volunteers: 1

Entry #53

Guaranteed Visitors

We are called to live a sacramental life, and in the life of the Church we are given many opportunities to expose our non-Orthodox friends and family to this sacramental life. During weddings, funerals, baptisms, and marriage blessings you are guaranteed to have visitors who are likely entering an Orthodox Church for the first time. Do not assume those receiving the sacrament are preparing their loved ones for the experience. We need to intentionally prepare ourselves and our visitors for what they are about to experience. Literature, a short homily, and preparatory emails to the participants are just a few ways we could make sure our visitors have an opportunity to properly experience the mystery they are about to witness. A couple getting married, grieving family members, and happy parents may be too focused on the event to realize that they need to prepare their loved ones for what is about to happen. I remember a priest of an older congregation telling me once that most of his visitors and catechumens come from funerals. The reverence we show our dead loved ones was so moving to these visitors that they wanted to know more. The same is true of every public service. The real question to answer for your visitors is this: are you putting the events in context? Answer this question and your visitors will become genuine enquirers.

- Time Required For Implementation: 3-6 months
- Implementation Cost: $0
- Ongoing Cost: $1 per visiting household in literature
- Required Volunteers: 1

Entry #54

Home Groups

During the 2010 Missions and Evangelism Conference of the Antiochian Archdiocese the Very Reverend Peter Gillquist, of blessed memory, talked about the implementation of home groups at his parish. The people reported that the home groups were some of the most meaningful events they experienced with church members. They promised to keep the evening short for those who had to pay for babysitting, which was usually two hours. Those who wanted to stay longer were allowed to. The groups were determined according to geography, but no one was forced to participate. After doing a short prayer service, the group would discuss the gospel reading for the coming Sunday. They would also have meaningful icebreakers by starting the night with an important question. One example Fr. Peter gave of the questions they used was, "what are you most afraid of?" Fr. Peter said the questions often provided all the content they needed for discussion, but having the night focused on the upcoming gospel kept everything in perspective and guaranteed a topic for discussion.

- Time Required For Implementation: 3-6 months
- Implementation Cost: $0
- Ongoing Cost: $0
- Required Volunteers: 2

Entry #55
Lending Library

This is similar to the bookstore, and should have at least the same categories as the bookstore: visitors, enquirers, catechumens, members. Growing a library is important. One way to grow your library is to have people donate books or sponsor the purchasing a book. St. Elias Orthodox Church in Atlanta, Georgia has an excellent library and borrowing system which was developed by John Truslow. If your jurisdiction has a distance education program preferred for ordination to the diaconate, I recommend having the required reading in your library. This will encourage people to enroll and stay in theological studies. John Truslow's article on starting a lending library first published in the *Word* magazine in 2001 is included as appendix J.

- Time Required For Implementation: 3-6 months
- Implementation Cost: $0 ask for book donations
- Ongoing Cost: $.50 per book for carbon-copy check out forms
- Required Volunteers: 1

Entry #56
Military Support

Americans love their military, and the Orthodox church prays for the military in every service. Care packages, especially during the holidays, communicate appreciation for our military. Consider other holidays, or all the holidays when deciding to send care packages. Also, Thanksgiving is close to Christmas and can be overlooked as an important holiday many soldiers are missing away from their families. A care package which includes some specific literature pertaining to the Orthodox Church may be the exact loving act which impacts the spiritual journey of a soldier. There are other ways to show appreciation besides care packages. The first is to establish a relationship with a local VA hospital, which falls under the category of doing good works in the community in the name of your church. You can also do a fundraiser specifically focused on the Wounded Warrior Project (www.woundedwarriorproject.org), such as a 5K race.

- Time Required For Implementation: 3-6 months
- Implementation Cost: $0
- Ongoing Cost: $5-10 per care package
- Required Volunteers: 2

Entry #57

Monastic Connection

This can be difficult because of the sparse locations, but having your parish develop a relationship with a monastery and a monastic will do wonders for the spiritual life of your parish. As one pastor put it, "I send off enquirer's to a weekend at a monastery and they come back with an Eastern ethos." This may be easier said than done depending on how close a monastery is. This exact experience happened to Fr. Mark Rowe, the Western Rite Dean for ROCOR in North America. While considering joining the Orthodox Church, it was his visit to a local monastery which made up his mind. America has a disconnect with the world of monastics, however much is being done to improve that.

- Time Required For Implementation: 3-6 months
- Implementation Cost: $0
- Ongoing Cost: $0-200 per trip
- Required Volunteers: 1

Entry #58
Nursing Home

Connecting with a nursing home can be similar to having a prison ministry. This will not result in automatic physical growth, and that is not why you are doing this. These people are unlikely to ever visit your church. Visiting the elderly, widows, and shut-ins is a Biblical commandment from Jesus. However, just like the prison ministry you will probably experience interest from the friends and family of those in the nursing home whom you are ministering to.

- Time Required For Implementation: 3-6 months
- Implementation Cost: $50 some nursing homes require background checks
- Ongoing Cost: $0
- Required Volunteers: 1

Entry #59

Oblate Program

The Order of St. Benedict offers an oblate program for those who find that they resonate with the monastic community but in reality should not live within one. The oblate membership is usually associated with a specific monastic community. An oblate program is an excellent event for a non-Orthodox Christian who is serious about their faith but looking for something deeper. St. Michael's in Whittier, California (the greater Los Angeles area) oblate program meet once a month for a rule of prayer, meditation, and then discussion. For more information about the oblates at St. Michael visit www.stmichaelwhittier.org/parish-site/about-our-parish/oblates. If you would prefer to establish an oblate program connected with a specific monastery visit www.christminster.org/oblates_vocations.html.

- Time Required For Implementation: 3-6 months
- Implementation Cost: $0
- Ongoing Cost: $0
- Required Volunteers: 1

Entry #60

Paid Youth Director

Fr. Evan Armatas, pastor of St. Spyridon's in Loveland, Colorado, hired a youth director before a church secretary. He said he could keep up with the administrative aspects of the church, but that the children needed a dedicated and accountable youth director. Paid youth director's focus on the future of your parish. They do not have to start out full-time. A large part of their time should be spent with the teenagers. Teenagers are not far from going off to college, which is the critical time we lose 60-80% of our youth. A paid youth director can help facilitate a healthy youth group where the teens have a sense of belonging in their home parish. This same youth director can be used to coordinate a local college group of Orthodox students and help them stay connect to the faith. A strong college group can be attractive to non-Orthodox students who are looking for deeper meaning. Some youth director's are just in charge of teens while others are overseeing the entire youth department from around 3 years old to 22.

- Time Required For Implementation: 3-6 months
- Implementation Cost: $0
- Ongoing Cost: $300-1,500 a month
- Required Volunteers: 1

Entry #61

Pregnancy Clinics

The Orthodox Church has always had a strong stance on anti-abortion. Consider establishing a relationship with a local maternity clinic which helps mothers avoid abortion. Connecting with these clinics is crucial because 9 out of 10 mothers who were intending to abort or considering an abortion change their mind after seeing an ultrasound. The ultrasound is one of the key ways a pregnancy clinic can show mothers that they are carrying a real baby, not a blob of flesh. Having a relationship with the clinic exposes the mothers to a healthy community (your church) available for them to join. For more information on helping young mothers visit www.zoeforlifeonline.org.

- Time Required For Implementation: 3-6 months
- Implementation Cost: $0
- Ongoing Cost: $0
- Required Volunteers: 1

Entry #62

Public Prayer

There are many efforts of public prayer already happening with Christians of different denominations coming together. The Greek Orthodox Archdiocese supports and explains this public prayer endeavor on their website. To learn more visit www.goarch.org/archdiocese/departments/outreach/observerarticles/renewal under the section called "Local Ecumenical Activites." A public week of prayer exists for Christian unity, See You At The Pole is another public prayer event happening at schools. There is also an active non-profit organization organizing 40 days of prayer and fasting in front of abortion clinics. As of the publication of this book, 59 abortion clinics have closed since the inception of this organization. For more information visit www.40daysforlife.com. The results section alone should grab your attention which can be found under the about section. Please note that whenever public prayer is happening alongside Christians from other denominations a priest needs to review the ecumenical guidelines from his jurisdictional clergy guide.

- Time Required For Implementation: 3-6 months
- Implementation Cost: $0
- Ongoing Cost: $0
- Required Volunteers: 2

Entry #63
St. Joseph's Guild

Many parishes struggle with getting the men involved in the life of the parish. I have visited too many churches where the women are teaching Sunday school, handling coffee hour, volunteering to clean the church, and helping in the church office. We have a prevalent problem across the American Orthodox Churches with a lack of men involved in the life of the parish. Fr. Victor Novak at Holy Cross Orthodox Church in Omaha, Nebraska, a ROCOR Western Right parish, started a St. Joseph's Guild. The guild is named after St. Joseph, the foster-father of Jesus, because of the work he did with his hands. This is "a group of woodworkers and craftsmen who work within the church. They have beautified our altar, built a credence table (necessary for Western Rite liturgics), done refinishing work on furnishings within the church, hung icons, etc. They serve the Temple with their gifts and talents and have been a tremendous blessing" (Fr. Viktor). The guild gathers all available men to come together for some tangible good works. These events are easy to coordinate and there is always work to be done. For more information on the structure and types of projects which can be done visit www.holycrossomaha.net.

- Time Required For Implementation: 3-6 months
- Implementation Cost: $0
- Ongoing Cost: $0
- Required Volunteers: 1

Entry #64

St. Hawaweeny Party

This idea was planted in my head by Bishop Thomas of the Antiochian Archdiocese, serving in the Diocese of Charleston, Oakland, and the Mid-Atlantic. The feast day of St. Raphael is next to Halloween in the Antiochian Archdiocese, and I am sure you can hear the linguistic similarities of Halloween and Hawaweeny. I am aware that the OCA has a different date of commemoration. Many churches are searching for a viable alternative for families not wanting to participate in traditional trick or treat (some neighborhoods and communities are fine while others focus on ghouls, goblins, witches and more). I recommend reading entry 67 (the next one) on a St. Nicholas Party for activity ideas. If weather permits, a trunk or treat can be just as fun for little ones as visiting homes in a neighborhood. The trunk or treat also allows you to station the activities in the form of a journey, having the children visit each trunk like one of St. Raphael's stops. If you have room in your parking lot have each vehicle be one of the specific 30 parishes St. Raphael established. Last, having someone dress up like St. Raphael and speaking Arabic through an interpreter can be fun for children as well. Make sure to include Brooklyn in one of the activities/games to emphasize where he was a bishop and where he died. Make sure to invite the community and announce this activity in the local paper.

- Time Required For Implementation: 3-6 months
- Implementation Cost: $500-1,500
- Ongoing Cost: should create profit
- Required Volunteers: 5-10

Entry #65
St. Nicholas Party

On the Saturday closest to St. Nicholas' Feast Day Holy Apostles Orthodox Church in Columbia, South Carolina of the OCA holds a party for children at the parish. It does not need to be long, anywhere from 2 hours before Vespers or for several hours around lunch time. Most churches keep it short, because it will need to be in doors. Having the celebration in doors limits the space, which limits the amount of activities. The St. Nicholas Day celebration I read about used almost the entire church (even the temple) with activity stations throughout the church for children to pick and choose activities. The priest would stay in the temple standing on the ambo dressed up as St. Nicholas. St. Nicholas probably spoke Greek, so if the priest learns a few Greek words it makes this part more interesting for the children. Have an interpreter there who will interpret questions the children have into Turkish for St. Nicholas. The interpreter has to know the answers because the priest and interpreter will not really be communicating. For the activities, make sure to focus on St. Nicholas. It can be easy to fill up the roster with Christmas events. It is good to have Christmas activities sprinkled throughout the church, but try to focus on St. Nicholas. There can be a place for children to color and make beards, have gold coin tosses, maybe even a short foot race in wooden shoes. Also, have all the children leave their shoes somewhere special when they arrive, and place gold coins in the shoes before they retrieve their shoes. Either before, during, or after, have someone tell the story of St. Nicholas. For more information visit www.stnicholasfestival.org.

- Time Required For Implementation: 3-6 months
- Implementation Cost: $500-1,500
- Ongoing Cost: should create profit
- Required Volunteers: 5-10

Entry #66

Specific Internal Fundraising

Fundraising is often more effective when raised for something specific. I once heard of someone announcing another letter from the bishop had arrived so pull out your wallets and purses. Sometimes this is how we feel about fundraising efforts for the church. However, if you specifically name what we are funding then all of the sudden people become generous. For example one church I visited needed some specific items for the altar. A parishioner from another church heard about the need and paid for the items. This parishioner was happy to buy the necessary items. If you are still unsure of this, research fundraising outside of the Orthodox Church and you will see this resonates with all successful efforts. If you need acolyte robes, then tell your congregation how many you need and how much each one costs. If your church needs a new roof, then tell your congregation about the bids you have received and the exact amount it will cost to repair the roof. Also, fundraising can be more specific if you show thanks to those who are giving (if they want the public appreciation).

- Time Required For Implementation: 3-6 months
- Implementation Cost: $0
- Ongoing Cost: $0
- Required Volunteers: 2

Entry #67
Vacation Bible/Church School

No matter which title you go with, make it fun, edifying, and something which your teens look forward to. I volunteered to run our VCS with zero knowledge of what to do several years ago. My experience was in summer camps so I asked for my pastor's blessing to turn the style of the week into a day camp. It was so similar in structure to the previous years of VCS that it was hard to see the difference leading up to the event. Even the curriculum was the same. All I did was change the style. It had been difficult to get the teens to sign up as volunteers during the planning phase. By the second day of VCS the teens were disappointed that they had not signed up to volunteer for the entire week because of how much fun they were having. The kids were saying this was the best it had ever been. Parents told us that kids were looking forward to it rather than trying to ditch. Once again all I did was change the style. We called it Camp Town and I incorporated as much as I could from the local diocesan camps in terms of programming. We even found someone in the church to design a t-shirt and gave a t-shirt to every child. If you want more information on this please contact me.

- Time Required For Implementation: 3-6 months
- Implementation Cost: $0
- Ongoing Cost: $250-1,500 per year, estimate $10 per child
- Required Volunteers: 5

Entry #68
Way Series

The Prophet Jonah Orthodox Church located in the Florida Keys offers the Way Series on a regular basis. The Way Series was developed by the Institute for Orthodox Christian Studies at Cambridge as an introduction to the Orthodox faith. The series lasts for 12 weeks. Each weekly session includes a meal, a talk on a Christian belief, a small group discussion, and a final segment where guests put questions to a panel. The Institute designed the Way Series to engage guests who have completed secondary school (more like a vocational school). Many churches around the world have hosted the course and have found it appealing to Christians seekers. The Prophet Jonah Church keeps information about the series on their website to attract visitors and enquirer's in the Florida Keys area. For more information visit www.iocs.cam.ac.uk/courses/courses_way.html.

- Time Required For Implementation: 3-6 months
- Implementation Cost: $49.95 (+ shipping) from Ancient Faith Publishing.
- Ongoing Cost: $0
- Required Volunteers: 6

Entry #69

Website

As part of my research for this book I have visited hundreds of Orthodox websites. A poor website is like an unkempt nave. It communicates a lack of care. A beautiful website communicates attention to detail and hospitality. In today's internet world the high majority of your visitors will explore your website before they physically visit the parish. There are plenty of good companies who provide graphic design for websites, but my favorite Orthodox based company is Logos Web Services. This is not to disparage any other provider. I am only providing my opinion. Also, here are some key elements I believe every parish website should have available in a clear and concise way. Our society has website expectations, so the following pieces need to be on your website: 1) Service Schedule: Visiting a parish website which has an old service schedule is more than frustrating. This lack of care tells people you do not want them to visit. 2) Contact Information: Most websites have this on there clearly, but they do not have a clear way of contacting the pastor. Even if the visitor needs to contact the pastor through the office, have that listed. 3) Clergy Information: A short biography about who the clergy are can make it easier for people to visit because they will begin to feel acquainted with the parish. 4) Photos: Have as many photos as possible of the church grounds, including temple, parish hall, Sunday school rooms, coffee hour, etc. This will also make it easier for visitors to find their way around. 5) Videos: YouTube is the second largest search engine on the internet. Not the second largest video search engine, the second largest search engine. As younger generations spend more time on the internet, videos are winning out over written content. Videos do not have to be created in high quality unless they are a promo video. Clips of services, coffee hour, and other events are fun to watch. Link to other videos which are well done and on public domain. For example, on myocn.net there is a wonderful video about St. Sophia's cathedral in California. The video was made by a visitor. Optional: I recommend broadcasting services over the internet. More and more churches are broadcasting their services, and this is great for several reasons. One is that homebound members can still participate. I would even explain the reason for the broadcasting is for your members who are not able to attend. 6) Optional: Consider having a page including information about the name of the parish, such as St. George or All Saints Of North America.

- Time Required For Implementation: 3-6 months
- Implementation Cost: $500-2,000
- Ongoing Cost: $150 annual
- Required Volunteers: 1

Part 3

6-12 Months

Entries 70 to 95

Entry #70

12 Baskets

This book contains many ideas which are feasible for you and many which will not work, but offer unto God that which He has given your church and He will return it blessed. For example, my church has 20 acres but we cannot build any more on it because of county septic codes. We could be frustrated about that restriction or focus on available resources. Tony Robbins says, "it's not about your resources, it's about your resourcefulness." While we cannot have any more building's with toilets, we can build other structures such as a ropes course or a pavilion. We also have a prayer chapel and icon stations scattered around the property. Resourcefulness is focusing on God's will, not your lack of resources.

- Time Required For Implementation: 6-12 months
- Implementation Cost: $0
- Ongoing Cost: $0
- Required Volunteers: 4

Entry #71

Antiphonal Chanting/Singing

St. Ignatius the God-Bearer, Bishop of Antioch, had a vision of angels singing antiphonally in heaven, alternate choirs worshipping God. A good choir is important, but antiphonal singing was given to us by a disciple of one of the apostles. This vision was so strong that St. Ignatius rearrange his church choir to perform antiphonally, and it became a common practice in the Orthodox Church. Antiphonal chanting is rare in America, and can resonate with visitors in a way other music does not. Not every church is prepared or equipped for this, but it can be as simple as two chanters stands instead of two choirs, one on the north side and one on the south. At All Saints Of North America Orthodox Church in Homer, Alaska they have a chanter's stand on the south side with men, and a chanter stand on the north side with women. If you are able to visit a church who has implemented this, you will then know why this entry is in this book.

- Time Required For Implementation: 6-12 months
- Implementation Cost: $0
- Ongoing Cost: $0
- Required Volunteers: 2

Entry #72

Climacus Conference

St. Michael Orthodox Church in Louisville, Kentucky hosts an annual conference open to the public. The conference has a different theme each year. Registration includes coffee, snacks, and all meals. It starts Friday afternoon and then continues throughout the day on Saturday. The conference is described as, "a classical Christian intellectual/spiritual event featuring scholars and voices across the fields of Theology, Philosophy, Classical Education, Literature, and History/Politics...enabling our ascension "of the ladder, as inspired by St. John Climacus and his *Ladder of Divine Ascent*." If you are in a community which enjoys theological and intellectual engagement, hosting a conference like this could be of great benefit to your church. For more information about the Climacus Conference visit www.climacusconference.org.

- Time Required For Implementation: 6-12 months
- Implementation Cost: $500-1000
- Ongoing Cost: should create some profit
- Required Volunteers: 4

Entry #73

Consignment Sale

St. Elizabeth Orthodox Church in Woodstock, GA held a consignment sale to raise funds and connect with the community. A consignment sale is where people bring their clothing, toys, and other items for resale. It is similar to a yard sale but also quite different. You probably have several parents in your parish currently participating in consignment sales, because they make clothing for children more affordable. Some sales will welcome all kinds of kids clothing while others focus on boutique brands. Things to consider include software, bar-coding systems, volunteer scheduling, and more. They usually last over several days and some can even last for two weeks. Most consignment sales happen twice a year to accommodate the changing of seasons. Typical numbers include 30% to the church from each sale, plus a $7-10 fee to help with advertising and other costs. Lowering the fee or percent in the beginning can help attract consignors.

- Time Required For Implementation: 6-12 months
- Implementation Cost: $0
- Ongoing Cost: should create profit
- Required Volunteers: 2

Entry #74
ESL Tutoring

We have many churches near or surrounded by a non-English speaking community. Many in that community want to learn English but do not know where to start or find help. You can hire someone with ESL training or pay for someone in the parish to go through the training. I do not have enough experience with ESL certification groups to recommend one, but getting certification provides the necessary training to host a successful ESL program.

- Time Required For Implementation: 6-12 months
- Implementation Cost: $100-500
- Ongoing Cost: $0
- Required Volunteers: 1

Entry #75

Festivals

Holy Ascension in Mt Pleasant, South Carolina hosts an unusual Orthodox festival every year. Fr. John Parker, Chair of the Department of Evangelism for OCA, is also the full-time pastor at Holy Ascension. Between the Greek Festival and the Russian Festival, Holy Ascension was struggling to find a way to offer a unique festival to the community. After some brainstorming the parish came up with a Music and Arts Festival. The festival is brilliant in several ways. First using the combination of music and art will attract a certain number of people who may not have been interested in visiting their parish otherwise. Also, this allows the parish to share their music and icons with the community. In addition, half of the vendors at the festival are not members of the church which gives the parish an opportunity to connect with them. The festival is relevant to Orthodoxy and yet does not rely on any ethnicities. This encourages everyone to participate and volunteer. During the festival tours are conducted for visitors by someone who can answer questions. If you are hosting a regular festival at your church or nearby, offer tours to the visitors. If your festival is held off-site, have a sign-up sheet for those who would like to visit the church for a tour. If you would like more information from Holy Ascension about their festival, visit their website at www.ocacharleston.org.

- Time Required For Implementation: 6-12 months
- Implementation Cost: $500-1,000
- Ongoing Cost: should create profit
- Required Volunteers: 10-20

Entry #76
GED Program

Many non-profit organizations and churches offer GED programs, but that is not a reason to think the market is saturated. The real question is this: how many in your community are doing it as ministry? The first process is contacting your state education system, because that is the controlling body for GEDs. Most states will also have regulations, licensing, and maybe some training requirements. This is another form of adult education, one which empowers the adults in your community to reach for higher goals. Creating a growth environment is essential to Orthodoxy and essential to your community. A GED program is a wonderful way to give back to and improve your community. Giving away fish is important in the meantime, but is rarely viable as a long term solution. Many states offer free classes and are looking for facilities to host the classes. Some states/counties will even provide the teachers if you will provide free space for them to teach. The generational positive impact this can have on a local community is almost unmeasurable. Contact your department of education for more information.

- Time Required For Implementation: 6-12 months
- Implementation Cost: state licensing
- Ongoing Cost: renewal of state licensing
- Required Volunteers: 1

Entry #77

Guest Speakers

A professional guest speaker can add energy and enthusiasm to a parish. It can also be a great event for members to invite non-Orthodox family, friends, and co-workers. If you are unsure of who to invite as a guest speaker, then I recommend checking two locations. The first is www.orthodoxspeakers.com. This was created by Kh. Frederica Mathewes-Green to provide a location for Orthodox churches to locate and utilize trustworthy speakers. You can read their bio and also search for a speaker by topic, such as evangelism, abortion, grief, or politics. Another place to find speakers is on internet radio such as Ancient Faith or OCN where you can listen to recorded presentations/homilies. When you have a guest speaker plan on recording them. Audio recordings are easier than video. If you record your guest speakers, then you will slowly build a library which can be shared and exchanged with other churches doing the same thing. A list of available speaking topics from the Orthodox Speakers Bureau is available as appendix K.

- Time Required For Implementation: 6-12 months
- Implementation Cost: travel & stipend
- Ongoing Cost: per visit
- Required Volunteers: 1

Entry #78

Homeschool Co-op

Home schooling is popular among many Orthodox families because of how many extra services we have throughout the year. There are many other good reasons to homeschool, and this is not an argument for or against home schooling children. If your parish has enough interested parents, consider hosting a homeschool co-op at the church. Most churches are empty during the week (unless there is some daycare) and are available as a great place for home school children to socialize. Fr. John Oliver at St. Elizabeth Orthodox Church in Murfreesboro, Tennessee has regular curriculum and teachers prepared for a weekly co-op session on Thursdays. Co-op curriculum may include church history, iconography, singing/chanting lessons, liturgical languages, and more. If you would like to talk to Fr. John about the co-op, the church office number is (615) 785-5285.

- Time Required For Implementation: 6-12 months
- Implementation Cost: $0
- Ongoing Cost: should break even by charging the cost to students
- Required Volunteers: parents of students on rotation

Entry #79

Mission Minded

Every parish could be supporting a seminarian and encouraging the congregation to go on missions trips like Project Mexico and YES. This support helps us get out of our little bubble and connect with Orthodoxy around the world. Seminarians always need financial help and are facing an uphill climb trying to pay bills while in school. Mission trips help us remember and help those less fortunate than we are. Mission trips humble us and seminarians help us to invest in our future. Another way to be mission minded is to adopt a mission who needs help. If your parish is doing well consider helping out a mission in your area.

- Time Required For Implementation: 6-12 months
- Implementation Cost: $0
- Ongoing Cost: every mission trip has a different cost
- Required Volunteers: 1

Entry #80
Movie & Discussion Panel

While I have not seen this implemented yet by an Orthodox Church, I know of several people discussing the idea and are close to implementing it. I will share the details which have been shared with me so far, although please be aware that there might be more changes and your particular resources may limit your options. The first obstacle is securing a local theatre screen. It was unanimously agreed upon that this was a better option than having this intentional engagement on a projector screen at the church. I have heard quotes anywhere from $300 to $1500 to rent out a theatre for several hours. Also, there is a requirement that for each Orthodox person attending there has to be one guest. The typical theatre will hold 150-300 people. So if a couple is attending from church, then each part of the couple should bring a friend. This allows for the maximum amount of attendance possible. I think you could have a contingency plan just in case the attendance looks low. The other way to increase attendance at an event like this is lower the cost of the tickets to something more affordable like $5 each. The next two decisions rely upon each other. You need to select a discussion panel and the movie to show. The discussion panel is available after the movie for questions about the movie and Orthodoxy. The panel would stand at the bottom in front of everyone similar to a college lecture style. I recommend having at least two or three people available, because you never know the difficulty of questions or range of interest. Also, this panel needs to be knowledgeable on the movie selected. Some ideas presented were the Russian movie *The Island*, Mel Gibson's *The Passion,* or one of the Narnia movies. Another one to consider is *I Am* by Tom Shadyac, or *The War Within*, narrated by Armand Assente.

- Time Required For Implementation: 6-12 months
- Implementation Cost: $300-1,500
- Ongoing Cost: same
- Required Volunteers: 2

Entry #81

On-Site Ministry

Establish a ministry located on the property such as a second hand clothing store, nursing home, food pantry, homeless shelter, or battered woman's shelter. St. George Orthodox Church in Orlando, Florida has a homeless ministry. St. George feeds and helps the local homeless on a daily basis. A ministry of this type usually comes when the church is established and has a little extra money they are trying to decide how to spend. We all have different resources (see the entry titled 12 Baskets). It is a great thing if your church becomes known for an on-site ministry.

- Time Required For Implementation: 6-12 months
- Implementation Cost: $0
- Ongoing Cost: $0
- Required Volunteers: 4

Entry #82
Outreach Brainstorming

One of the most valuable resources for growing an Orthodox Church is to form a group of people who come together to intentionally brainstorm on ways to connect to the community and be more present. No one knows your community the way your congregation does, so pick out some creative people combined with some grounded members and hash out some ideas. The creative people will bring the ideas and the grounded members will hash out the details and reality of your resources. Also, choose someone to conduct the meeting who is not necessarily in charge. This person would have the responsibility of conducting effective meetings and will keep things moving along. The Department of Stewardship, Outreach, and Evangelism of the Greek Orthodox Archdiocese of North America released a booklet on this topic titled *Outreach & Evangelism: Practical Steps*. For a copy of the booklet visit www.goarch.org/archdiocese/departments/outreach.

- Time Required For Implementation: 6-12 months
- Implementation Cost: $0
- Ongoing Cost: $0
- Required Volunteers: 4

Entry #83

Parish Council Reorientation

The parish council is a ministry. Fr. Nicholas Trianfalou held his meetings in the nave, because if it can't be held there then the members are forgetting their ministry. Fr. Alexander Addy, of blessed memory, required regular participation in the life of the church to be on the parish council. This includes participation in the services, sacraments, etc. Also, he required each member to go through training to be on the council. He never had an empty parish council seat because his parish knew how important that ministry was. If you are having problems filling offices, then make sure to encourage the entire congregation to visit the parish council meetings. If you are not allowing your congregation to visit the meetings, then maybe there is a problem. Many other churches post their minutes and financials in the parish hall for the congregation to see. This public posting creates trust and accountability. Some time ago a priest, and I wish I could remember who it was, said he did away with committees. All reports given at the Parish Council Meeting are on ministries of the parish. This renaming helped the members realize the importance of the work they were doing for their own church. Last is to have a term limit. Deciding on the length of term is not important if there is no term limit. Term limits keep church leadership from becoming complacent. The longest I have heard someone should be a parish council president is eight years, most preferring something closer to five. Term limits inspire ambition and goals with deadlines.

- Time Required For Implementation: 6-12 months
- Implementation Cost: $0
- Ongoing Cost: $0
- Required Volunteers: 1

Entry #84

Presentations From Organizations

Each jurisdiction in North America has a list of ministries and organizations it has endorsed/worked with. You can also find a list of ministries and endorsed organizations at The Assembly of Bishop's website: www.assemblyofbishops.org. Reach out to each organization and tell them they are welcome to come and make presentations. Some will need help with travel costs while others will come at their own expense. A short list of organizations to consider includes: IOCC, OCMC, OCF, Ancient Faith Radio, OCN, FOCUS (and Yes), camping programs, seminaries, and St. Katherine's Or Hellenic College/Holy Cross Orthodox colleges. Presentations from the previous organizations or others are great events to invite non-Orthodox friends and family to.

- Time Required For Implementation: 6-12 months
- Implementation Cost: $0 if they come at their own expense
- Ongoing Cost: $0
- Required Volunteers: 1

Entry #85

Prison Ministry

This one is explicitly in the Bible: Matthew 25:36. A prison ministry will not directly result in more visitors to your parish, but it will indirectly get friends and family of the inmates you are ministering to interested in your joyful Christian community. Also, this is a good time to learn the difference between prison and jail. Prisons are more of a long-term facility and usually run by state and federal governments. Jails are typically short-term facilities and run at a local county or city level. If you are looking to help inmates who will be released soon, you should focus on county jails. For more resources and ideas visit www.theocpm.org, which is an agency of the Assembly of Bishops of North America. "The Orthodox Church has dedicated the 6th Sunday of Pascha as the official day to recognize prison ministry in every Orthodox parish around the United States." For ideas on homilies for 2015 see appendix L. Each year OCPM puts out new ideas for homilies.

- Time Required For Implementation: 6-12 months
- Implementation Cost: $0
- Ongoing Cost: $5 per inmate for curriculum
- Required Volunteers: 1

Entry #86

Scouting Groups

The Boy Scouts have received much attention and criticism over the past few years. There are still many Christian organizations and even Orthodox Churches sponsoring and hosting scouting troops. Fortunately our bishops formed a committee many years ago focused on the ministry of scouting. For more information visit www.eocs.org. This committee even has four awards available related to Eastern Orthodox Scouting. For example, the Eagle Scout project has benefitted our church several times with new fencing, remodeling, and more. Scouting is important to the Orthodox, because we realize the importance of God's creation and spending time with it. Throughout the Bible and history great Christians, including Jesus, went into nature to spend time in prayer. Scouting teaches valuable lessons related to nature and God's creation, and specifically having a troop at your church can have a strong and lasting impression on your youth. Consider all the different troops: boys scouts, girl scouts, cub scouts, etc.

- Time Required For Implementation: 6-12 months
- Implementation Cost: $0
- Ongoing Cost: $0
- Required Volunteers: 3

Entry #87

Service Books

If you do not have volunteers available to sit with visitors, or even if you do, try to have updated and current service books. If the content of the service book does not match at least 90% of what is being said during the service, then consider getting new books. Christ The Savior Orthodox Church in Anderson, South Carolina printed their own books. The good news is that printing your own service books is affordable. Having it typed and formatted for printing can be tedious. If you save your work, then making future changes will be simple and easy. We create confusion for our guests when we are trying to explain extra segments not in the service book or skipping over portions. There are enough confusing experiences for a guest to a Divine Liturgy. We have the ability and responsibility to remove the confusion surrounding service books.

- Time Required For Implementation: 6-12 months
- Implementation Cost: $0
- Ongoing Cost: $5-10 per book
- Required Volunteers: 1

Entry #88

Signage

Almost every church I visit has a beautiful sign if you are standing 10 feet away. These same signs are difficult to read and understand if driving by at 30 mph or faster. For your church sign consult a sign company on design, information, and colors. Only put the most relevant information which can be read while driving by at 30 mph (or whatever the speed limit is on your parish's street). The basics should be present in your sign: name, phone number, address, and website. Just those items will be difficult to read if the colors are soft or the text size is too small. The other signage needed is on the church grounds and inside the church. Make sure there are clear signs to the church office for visitors. Make sure there are clear signs to the front doors of the temple from the parking lot. A lot of people will arrive extra early or late when visiting and will not have people to follow in. Also, have clear signs to restrooms and coffee hour from the narthex.

- Time Required For Implementation: 6-12 months
- Implementation Cost: $100-5,000
- Ongoing Cost: $0
- Required Volunteers: 1

Entry #89

Spiritual Gifts

Under the guidance of a spiritual father (or mother) discover your spiritual gift from God to be used for His glory and the glorification of His church. Each person is given a different gift. The gift can be used for personal gain or to glorify God. For example my wife was given the gift of discernment (and yet somehow married me!). I did not discover my gift until I was in my thirties. "God has appointed these in the church: first apostles, second prophets, third teachers, after that miracles, then gifts of healings, helps, administrations, varieties of tongues" (1 Corinthians 12:28). I am not an authority on spiritual gifts, but I do know the Orthodox approach on gifts is that we all as individuals make up the body of Christ, and our individualism can be used to grow the church. A basic way to consider this can be found in a book called *The E-Myth* by Michael Gerber. Gerber breaks down the employment world into three categories: entrepreneurs, managers, and technicians. Learning who you are helps you properly apply the gifts God has given you. Another tool which may help in this area is personality testing, such as Myers-Briggs. Myers-Briggs helped me discover my spiritual gift.

- Time Required For Implementation: 6-12 months
- Implementation Cost: $0
- Ongoing Cost: $0
- Required Volunteers: 2

Entry #90
Sunday School

This is important for two reasons. One reason is that for families only partially involved in the church this may be the only Christian Education some children are receiving. Making the gospel relevant in their lives could make the difference in how seriously they take their faith when older. Also, Sunday School can also effect whether families visit a second time. The protestant world in America has made Sunday School a necessity, and without it a visiting family may wonder where the priorities are of your parish. Keep in mind, if you are having Sunday School on a different day, such as Tuesday night, make sure you guests are aware of this. Many churches are embracing a new program called Catechesis of the Good Shepherd, which has been adopted and adjusted from a Roman Catholic program of the same name.

- Time Required For Implementation: 6-12 months
- Implementation Cost: $100-1,000
- Ongoing Cost: $10-100
- Required Volunteers: 3

Entry #91
Tithe

There are factual, historical justifications why many churches have been on a dues system, but the truth is that in America dues are no longer needed and go against the tradition of Orthodoxy. Tithing is our tradition and is older than the Orthodox Church. Tithing can be found in both the Old and New Testaments and has generally been accepted to mean 10%. Tithing is us giving 10% of God's money back to Him in appreciation for what He has given us. If you church is currently not on a tithing system, sometimes it can be better to have an outsider come and make a presentation on stewardship, with tithing being one of the key aspects.

- Time Required For Implementation: 6-12 months
- Implementation Cost: $0
- Ongoing Cost: $0
- Required Volunteers: 2

Entry #92
Tourist/Travel Resources

The Chamber of Commerce will usually have tourist information for those traveling through town. Sometimes it is free and sometimes it costs money, but put your parish down as one of the must-sees of the town. Most people have never visited an Orthodox Church and are unaware of the beauty inside. Have "tourists" information ready, because they are probably visiting your church for non-religious reasons. Some transportation departments will allow you to pay to be on a sign saying, "St. (blank) Orthodox Church: 100 Miles," and have official road signs from the highway pointing to your location. Make your church a destination. Be prepared to keep the doors of the temple unlocked if you are going to try this entry. Some churches are able to do this while others have to keep their doors locked.

- Time Required For Implementation: 6-12 months
- Implementation Cost: $30-100
- Ongoing Cost: $30-100 annually
- Required Volunteers: 1

Entry #93

TV Show

Fr. Philip Rogers, pastor of The Archangel Gabriel Orthodox Church, hosts an Orthodox TV show on the local access channel in Lafayette, Louisiana. The beginning structure of the show included an epistle reading, a Gospel reading, a sermon, and if time allows they talked about the saint of the day. Now they are giving presentations during the show on other topics, such as the Nicene Creed. The cost was $50 a year, and they had to wait awhile to secure a prime time spot. While the newest episodes are not uploaded to youtube on a regular basis, there is a new episode every Thursday evening at 8 PM airing for the public to see. Entry level video editing software is available for free for both Windows and Mac users. For more information or to watch the videos visit www.stgabrielorthodox.org.

- Time Required For Implementation: 6-12 months
- Implementation Cost: $500 for camcorder, lapel mic, tripod
- Ongoing Cost: $50 per year
- Required Volunteers: 2

Entry #94

Weekday Childcare

I am familiar with three types of weekday childcare: pre-school, daycare, and mothers morning out. Most churches start with a mother's morning out. If you are unsure about structure, times, and cost, then research any churches already offering weekday childcare in your area. The benefits of starting with mother's morning out is that you can offer it just one or two days a week until you see that it will be beneficial. Most churches do a suggested donation, but you can also make it free if you want to. You would need to do a legal check with child services to see if you are allowed to definitively charge a fee instead of a suggested donation. Daycare would be the next step up from mother's morning out. A mother's morning out program can be anywhere from 2-4 hours, while daycare can last all day. Each state department has different regulations on childcare. For example childcare in Tennessee which is less than six hours a day has fewer regulations than those which are six hours or longer. Therefore, a local preschool in my area has childcare available for five and a half hours. Pre-school is the final and most intense option for weekday childcare. While many would agree that having an Orthodox pre-school around is beautiful and a blessing, many state departments will allow for some type of religious curriculum even within a daycare without all the regulations of a preschool. If you resources allow for a preschool then I definitely recommend it. For example, St. John's Cathedral in Eagle River, Alaska runs a preschool and grade school but they are in a separate building from the church.

- Time Required For Implementation: 6-12 months
- Implementation Cost: $100-1,00
- Ongoing Cost: should create profit if you accept donations
- Required Volunteers: 2

Entry #95

Weekend Seminar

Fr. Aidan Wilcoxson at St. John the Forerunner Orthodox in Cedar Park, Texas runs a weekend seminar twice a year designed for members to bring their non-Orthodox friends and family. Randomly bringing guests to a church service without preparation can be quite damaging, and sometimes our friends and family need to hear about Orthodoxy from someone else. The seminar starts Friday evening with a presentation on Church history followed by a presentation on Holy Tradition. If you are interested in this idea keep in mind that it can take a few years to build momentum and buzz around the public event throughout your community. For more information about the seminar visit www.theforerunner.org.

- Time Required For Implementation: 6-12 months
- Implementation Cost: $0
- Ongoing Cost: $500-1,000 per seminar for guest speakers and advertising
- Required Volunteers: 3

Part 4

1-5 Years

Entries 96-100

Entry #96

Deacons, Sub-deacons, and Readers

Deacons, sub-deacons, and readers all have a unique and necessary part in the liturgical life of the church. Fr. Alexander Schmemann said the following about deacons in his book *The Eucharist*, "We can already note that if in our day the presence of a deacon in *every* church community has ceased to be perceived as necessary and self-evident, as one of the conditions of the *fullness* of church life, and the "diaconate" has been converted into a certain "decorative" appendage...then is that not because the experience of the Church herself as the love of Christ and the liturgy as the expression and fulfillment of that love has been weakened in us, if not entirely dissipated?" (Schmemann p.108) Each has a part to play and they each need to know their part and perform it with reverence and holiness. The diaconate was the first official office of the church, with more descriptions on it than others in the New Testament. The sub-deacon has been around longer than the New Testament and has a dedicated ministry to the Bishop and to the care of the temple. The reader provides us with volume, enunciation, and pronunciation of our sacred hymns. Have you ever visited a church without a protopsalti? You will notice a difference in preparation, organization, and execution of the services. Having these roles properly filled will have a positive effect on visitors. Church leadership is not just the priest and the parish council. Every aspect of church life is a ministry and every ministry needs a leader. This entry falls under 1-5 years because of the amount of time it takes for a person to be considered for ordination to reader or sub-deacon, and most jurisdictions require three or four years of training to be a deacon.

- Time Required For Implementation: 1-5 years
- Implementation Cost: $0 (diaconal programs vary in cost)
- Ongoing Cost: $0
- Required Volunteers: 3

Entry #97

Health & Wellness Services

I know of two churches (and there are probably several more) who have established health clinics in their church. They are also able to offer wellness seminars to the public. One of the clinics is located at the FOCUS center in Pittsburgh, Pennsylvania, "a free medical and behavioral health clinic for people who are uninsured or who don't qualify for medical assistance." The FOCUS center also houses a new Orthodox mission. For more information on the FOCUS clinic in Pittsburgh, PA visit www.focuspittsburgh.org. There is another clinic at Holy Trinity Greek Orthodox Church in Nashville, TN. Holy Trinity established the clinic in the name of St. Sampson the Hospitable. The focus of the clinic is to provide rheumatology care to the uninsured. Visits are only $10. For more information on the St. Sampson clinic visit www.stsampsonclinic.com. If you are considering offering a health seminar or health care services, contact all of your local Orthodox churches to search for medical personnel who may want to help. This could be a great opportunity to create a Pan-Orthodox ministry in your local community. Another idea is to have nurses from the parish visit the homes of parishioners who are either temporarily or permanently home-bound. Home-bound parishioners can benefit emotionally and medically from a visiting nurse of the local church.

- Time Required For Implementation: 1-5 years
- Implementation Cost: $0 if you focus on fundraising
- Ongoing Cost: same
- Required Volunteers: 3

Entry #98

Orthodox Natural Church Development (ONCD)

ONCD is a two year process which begins with a survey to determine the health of your parish before considering how to grow it. Fr. Jonathan Ivanoff, the Director of ONC, makes sure the process is detailed, organized, and professional. The priest selects 30 active members, or as many as possible if 30 are not available, to do a series of surveys. The surveys identify the growth areas needing the most attention. The surveys also provide a clear map for the next several years of what to focus on. The testimonials should be encouraging to any pastor who is not sure what to do next. ONCD focuses on quality, not quantity. The goal is to make sure the church is healthy and spiritually feeding everyone. For more information visit www.oncd.us. If you are unfamiliar with the growing problem of unfed spiritual children in our Orthodox churches, then please consider reading an article by Dr. Bradley Nassif about the revolving door in American Orthodox Churches. The article is located in appendix M.

- Time Required For Implementation: 1-5 years
- Implementation Cost: depends on amount of consulting
- Ongoing Cost: $2000-$3000
- Required Volunteers: 20

Entry #99

Staff Therapist

Not every priest is trained in counseling. The ideal situation is to have a pastor trained in pastoral counseling, and training in Marriage & Family Therapy is available from the Antiochian Archdiocese for all clergy. Clergy should also consider training as a Pastoral Care Specialist. However, if the pastor is not trained and is not interested in being trained please consider having an on-site professional counselor. The counselor does not need to be full-time, and may even be willing to donate the time. The counselor does need to be professionally trained. Professional counselors are trained to handle situations the rest of us can enable or make worse. The only thing that might be more important than pastoral counseling is pastoral care. I recommend having a suggested donation for visitors who are not Orthodox, while members should be encouraged to donate whatever they can.

- Time Required For Implementation: 1-5 years
- Implementation Cost: $0-40,000
- Ongoing Cost: $0-40,000 annually
- Required Volunteers: 1

Entry #100

Start A Mission

An established church should consider starting a mission if they are stagnant but have financial resources. Roughly every five years an established church could be helping to start a mission. Maybe that mission is nearby or maybe it is somewhere else inside the state. It should only take five years for a mission to become established if there is a mother church helping it intentionally and has a plan for that mission. A great resource for starting a mission can be found at the OCA website in the form of a pdf handbook: www.oca.org/cdn/PDFs/evangelization/2005-Evangelization-Hndbk.pdf. You could also consider giving them a copy of this book!

- Time Required For Implementation: 1-5 years
- Implementation Cost: funds for commercial space and temple items
- Ongoing Cost: monthly expenses
- Required Volunteers: depends on the jurisdiction. 10 tithing households should be able to support a full-time priest.

Appendix A
Entry #2
Antidoron Recipe

Prosphora means "that which is offered." In the Orthodox Church, this is the term used for the bread which is offered for the celebration of the Divine Liturgy. From this bread will be taken a portion which, during the Liturgy, becomes the Body of Christ. It is therefore most important that the Prosphora not only be properly prepared but that the person or family preparing it be in a spiritual frame of mind. It is suggested that the person or family designated to bake the Holy Bread do the following:

- Make sure that during the time you have designated to bake, you are free from unnecessary distractions, that you do not become provoked or irritated.
- Make sure that the Prosphora be prepared in a neat, clean, and orderly surrounding and atmosphere.
- Make sure that after all the ingredients (flour, yeast, pans, etc.) have been gathered, you pray the Prayers to Be Said Prior to the Making of the Prosphora. After these prayers have been said, begin combining the ingredients.
  - PRAYER BEFORE MAKING THE PROSPHORA: Almighty God, our Help and Refuge, Fountain of Wisdom and Tower of Strength, who knows that I can do nothing without Your guidance and help; assist me, I pray Thee, and direct me to divine wisdom and power, that I may prepare this prosphora, faithfully and diligently, according to Thy will, so that it may be profitable to myself and others, and to the glory of Thy Holy Name. For thine is the Kingdom and the power and the glory of the Father, and of the Son and of the Holy Spirit, now and ever and unto ages of ages. Amen.
- Some traditions have a lit candle and icon present during the making of the Prosphora.

INGREDIENTS AND EQUIPMENT: This recipe makes six loaves. Make the full recipe; any extra loaves should be placed in the parish hall freezer.

5 ½ cups warm water

3 tablespoons yeast

5 ½ to 6 teaspoons salt

15 cups flour (5 lb. bag) – unbleached, plain flour

6 pans

Bread Seal

Large ziplock bags

Parchment Paper

Toothpicks

Stiff Brush

Pillowcase

Place warm water in a large bowl. Sprinkle the yeast into the warm water and stir until dissolved. In a separate bowl, put about 12 cups of flour and add the salt to the flour and stir. Gradually add this flour/salt mixture, 1-2 cups at a time into the water/yeast mixture. Continue adding flour until you can't add any more and take the dough out of the bowl and knead in as much flour as needed to make a stiff dough (for a total of up to 15 cups). Knead for 10-15 minutes or until the dough is smooth and elastic, has no lumps, and no longer sticks to the work surface.

Divide the dough into six parts (I shape the dough like a loaf of bread and then use a serrated knife to cut into six parts). Place parchment paper in the pan (this does not need to be cut perfectly, it can be cut in a square and raise up from the sides) or you may flour the pans but DO NOT USE PAM OR VEGETABLE OIL.

Take one section of dough and knead in a little more flour and flatten with hands to make a circle. (I smack it hard to get out any air bubbles). Place in the pan and put a light dusting of flour on top. You do not need to flour the seal. Press the seal firmly into the loaf. While still holding the seal down, use a toothpick to make holes all around the perimeter of the seal (as shown in the diagram below). Pull the seal straight up and poke additional holes around the seal imprint (as shown in the diagram below). The holes are important so that there are no air pockets or bubbles. Use the brush to brush off excess flour on the seal before pressing into each additional loaf.

Let rise for about 30 minutes. Bake at 325 degrees for 40-45 minutes. This long baking time is **ESSENTIAL TO THE SUCCESS OF THE BREAD**. If the bread is undercooked in the center (which is often the case with a shorter baking time), it is very difficult for the celebrating priest to remove the Lamb (the middle portion) for use in the Eucharist. Ovens may vary but **it is much better to overcook than to undercook.** It should sound hollow when tapped and the degree of "brownness" will vary.

Remove baked bread from oven and remove from pans immediately. Dust all excess flour off with brush and wrap in white towels and place in the pillowcase provided. **(Note: Do not wash the towels or pillowcase with bleach or fabric softener – it severely affects the taste of the bread).** After the bread has cooled completely, put in individual zip lock bags.

PRAYER AFTER THE BREAD IS BAKED: Dear Lord, this bread that I have baked represents each one in my family and in my congregation. I am offering myself to You, my very life, in humble obedience and total commitment to You. I place myself on Your holy altar through this bread to be used by You in any way that You feel will help enlarge Your kingdom. Accept my gift and make me worthy to receive the greater gift that You will give me when You consecrate this bread and give it back to me as Your Precious Body. Amen.

Bring the loaves and your completed prayer list to the church no later than **9:00 a.m. on Sunday**. The priest must have them in order to perform the proskomedia service.

On the last day that you are responsible to bring the bread, please bring the basket of equipment to the church to be given to the next person on the rotation. Call the next person on rotation to remind them. Generally you will be scheduled to prepare the bread for two consecutive Sundays. If by chance a special service falls between those two Sundays, you may be asked to prepare the prosphora for the third service.

Please follow these instructions precisely. Please do not make changes. If you have any questions, you can contact _____. Also, if something is missing or needs to be replaced in the basket, please notify me.

Appendix B
Entry #9
Christmas Carols

1. Away In A Manger
2. Hard The Herald Angels Sing
3. It Came Upon A Midnight Clear
4. Joy To The World
5. O Come All Ye Faithful
6. O Holy Night
7. O Little Town of Bethlehem
8. Silent Night

Appendix C
Entry #11
Restroom Checklist

- Toilet paper stocked per toilet. Keep extra rolls in the stall.
- Toilets flushed.
- Stall doors latch.
- Floors clean, no trash or spills.
- Counters clean, wipe down and keep dry.
- Sinks & faucets clean.
- Mirrors clean, no spots.
- Soap dispenser stocked, no spills.
- Paper towels stocked or air dryers cleaned.
- Trash can emptied if 75% full or more.
- Pleasant fragrance, install air fresheners.
- Light bulbs all working.
- Cleaner available nearby.
- Keep the trashcan by the door if you can.

Appendix D
Entry #13
Orthodox Camping Programs
(alphabetical by state/province)

All information taken from www.orthodoxcamps.org/directory except for Alaska.

- Alaska
    - St. John's Summer Camp, Antiochian. (http://www.stjohnalaska.org/summercamp.html)
- Alberta
    - Camp St. Innocent, Antiochian.
- Arizona
    - All Saints Pan-Orthodox Summer Camp, Greek.
- British Columbia
    - All Saints of North America Orthodox Youth Camp, OCA.
- California
    - Ascension Cathedral Camp, Greek.
    - Camp St. Nicholas, Antiochian.
    - Camp St. Sava, Serbian.
    - St. Eugene's Summer Camp, OCA.
    - St. Nicholas Ranch & Retreat Center, Greek.
    - St. Sophia Camp, Greek.
- Colorado
    - Camp Emmanuel, Greek.
- Georgia
    - St. Seraphim and St. Sophia Camps, OCA.
- Florida
    - Camp St. Stephen, Greek.
- Idaho
    - Camp St. Mary of Egypt, Antiochian.
- Illinois
    - Camp Fanari, Greek.
    - ORPR Camp, ROCOR.
- Indiana
    - St. John's Camp, OCA.
- Iowa
    - Camp St. George, Antiochian.
- Kansas
    - Eastern Orthodox Youth Camp, OCA.

- Maryland
    - CYC Summer Camp, Greek.
- Michigan
    - Camp Vatra for Juniors and Seniors, OCA.
    - Metropolis of Detroit Summer Camp, Greek.
    - St. Nicholas Summer Camp, Greek.
- Minnesota
    - St. Mary's Church Camp, Greek.
- New Hampshire
    - Metropolis of Boston Camp, Greek.
    - New England Youth Rally, OCA.
- New York
    - Camp St. Paul, Greek.
    - Ionian Village, Greek.
    - St. Andrew's Camp, OCA.
    - St. Timothy's Summer Camp, Greek.
- Ohio
    - St. Vladimir's Camp, OCA.
- Oklahoma
    - Camp St. Raphael, Antiochian.
- Oregon
    - Camp Angelos Youth Camp, Greek.
- Pennsylvania
    - All Saints Camp, Ukrainian.
    - Antiochian Village, Antiochian.
    - Camp Good Shepherd, Greek.
    - Camp Nazareth, American Carpatho-Russian.
    - Metropolis of Pittsburgh Summer Camp at Camp Nazareth, Greek.
    - St. Sava Camp, Serbian.
    - St. Tikhon's Summer Camp, OCA.
- Saskatchewan
    - Camp St. Nicholas, OCA.
- South Carolina
    - Camp St. Thekla, Antiochian.
- Washington
    - All Saints Camp, Greek.
- Wisconsin
    - Chicago Deanery Camp, OCA.
    - St. Mary's Camp, OCA.

Appendix E
Entry #18
Evangelism Homily 1 of 10

This sermon is also available as an audio recording at:
http://www.ancientfaith.com/podcasts/emmaus/lenten_evangelism_1_the_pub lican_and_pharisee_sermon_feb._1_2015

Sunday of the Publican and the Pharisee, February 1, 2015
Rev. Fr. Andrew Stephen Damick

In the Name of the Father and of the Son and of the Holy Spirit, one God. Amen.

We now begin the pre-Lenten period with the Sunday of the Publican and Pharisee. Today is the day we open the Triodion, the liturgical book that governs this time of year. And this year, we will be doing something new on these Sundays both before and during Great Lent—the sermons will all fall into a series with a single theme. This is not something I've done before, so I hope you will bear with me if this is a little experimental.

And so what is the theme? For the next ten weeks, from today through Palm Sunday, we will be discussing evangelism. Each Sunday of the Triodion has a different theme to it, usually based in the Gospel reading, and all of them have something to say about sharing the good news of Jesus Christ to the world. The Gospel is like a great jewel with many facets, each sparkling with its own light, and each drawing us into the depths of the beauty of this most precious gift. So from now until Palm Sunday, we will be looking at different facets of this gem of evangelism.

This Sunday, we read the Gospel parable of the Publican and the Pharisee. And the overall theme here is humility. It is the Publican, this tax collector and infamous sinner, whose prayer before God justifies him, that is, puts him into a right relationship with the Lord. And it is the Pharisee, known for his sanctity and exact observance of the tenets of his faith, whose prayer is only "with himself," as the Scripture says, and it fails to provide him with justification before God.

The lesson here is clear enough—be humble. The fervent prayer of a humble heart reconciles us to God, justifying us even if we are great sinners. And this apparently righteous man, the Pharisee, who leads a good life and does what he is supposed to—he goes away from his prayer unjustified.

So how does this connect with our theme of evangelism?

One of the dangers that many Christians fall into is seeing the purpose of the local parish as being almost exclusively about taking care of the people who are already there. Often, when this kind of approach to church life is made central, we hear the phrase "our people" or "our own" a lot. With this view, if someone mentions emphasizing outreach, there is often a backlash of fear that such an emphasis would mean that "our people" would become neglected. And Christians and even whole parishes turn inward and become about trying to hold on to what they have.

But this is actually a distortion of church life. We have to recall how it is that Church life began—it began with the descent of the Holy Spirit at Pentecost, filling the disciples of Jesus with power from on high, power that they immediately began to use to preach the Gospel to any who would listen. And they were fulfilling the last command that the Lord Jesus gave before His ascension, to go into all the world and preach the Gospel to every creature, to baptize them in the Name of the Father, Son and Holy Spirit, and to teach them to do all that He had commanded.

This same kind of distortion exists on the individual level, too, and we sometimes use parables like the Publican and Pharisee to try to justify it. I only need to become humble, to work on my own spiritual life, to cultivate myself and what I have, and that is my purpose here. I have spiritual needs, and here I get them met. I come here to pray, and this faith exists to serve my spiritual needs and the needs of my family and friends. It is all very inward focused.

What we do not realize when we fall prey to this temptation is that this attitude actually has nothing at all to do with the humility taught by the Publican. And to understand why, we have to ask why he was repenting, what his prayer was about. The Publican is a public sinner. He is someone who has harmed other people. And so when he asks God for mercy, he does so precisely with the knowledge that he has been causing pain for other people. He has been taking from them what is theirs and keeping it for his own. His repentance is not some private spiritual experience. His repentance is part of the process of healing his relationship with his community.

So we see now what this has to do with evangelism. To bring the good news to the world, we have to have humility. And what is humility? It is to place ourselves last and always to place someone else first.

If I take humility as a true principle for what it means to be an Orthodox Christian, then everything changes for me. I come here not to ask what this parish can do for me, how it can serve me—which is really just a way of asking how God can serve me, because this parish is nothing other than an outpost of His Kingdom. Instead, I come asking how I can serve God. I come here asking for Him to have mercy on me, because it is I who am the sinner. I come here asking to be let in and made a citizen of His Kingdom, because I do not deserve it. I have done nothing to deserve it. The only ticket into this Kingdom is mercy. And mercy is for those who are repentant sinners. Mercy is for the humble.

And when I ask what I can do to serve, then I become focused not on my own spiritual needs, my own desires, but I become focused on what the needs are of those around me, both within the parish and those who belong to this parish but are not in this parish. And I don't mean only those whose names are on the membership rolls but are not present here today—though I do mean them—but also those who live here in our community but have not yet seen the light of Christ here.

For they are also members of this parish. They also belong here. There are so many who are ready to respond if only one of us would love them and bring them here, if only one of us would make it our mission to pray for them, if only one of us would see their pain and their abandonment and their confusion and bring them the light.

They also belong to us, and we are like wicked publicans if we do not bring them what we owe them. We have been entrusted with the greatest treasure the world has ever seen, a treasure that belongs to all mankind, a treasure given by God Himself when He became one of us, and yet most of us prefer to keep that treasure to ourselves. When we do that, we are wicked publicans who steal from our own people, in collusion not with the Roman Empire but with the principalities and powers of darkness, who would see us all remain in spiritual destitution.

If we have humility, then we cannot help but evangelize. We cannot help but bring the good news to our family, our friends, our neighbors, our co-workers, our fellow students, and so on and on until every last person we know has been invited into this holy place to see the Face of God and to hear His voice, and to know the power and the glory and the rest and the healing and the love of our Savior Jesus Christ.

So does this mean that we forget about the people who are here and spend all our time trying to get new people here? By no means. What it means is that we transform our vision for who we are as Orthodox Christians, for who we are as St. Paul Antiochian Orthodox Church of Emmaus, into a vision of humility and love. If we do that, then our outreach will also find those same people whom we worry about who are no longer here or who are only occasionally here or who are here and hurting in our midst, perhaps unknown to us, silent in their suffering and in their need.

The ministry of this holy church does not belong only to the clergy or the choir or the parish council or any of our active organizations—it belongs to each of us and to all of us. God is calling me right now like the Publican to humble myself, to pray for His mercy, to commit or recommit myself to the preaching of the good news of Jesus Christ to every creature, to ask not where I can be served but where I can serve.

This feeling that the Church exists to serve me, this distortion of church life, is hidden in many wounded hearts throughout the holy Orthodox Church, and the hearts of the saints cry out to God with the Prophet King David "How long, O Lord, how long?" And they wait for us to awaken, to see that the whole world is our parish, and to humble ourselves and pray for God's mercy for our sin. And they wait for us to see that the only way our own spiritual needs can be met is by asking how we can serve others. Because if we only look to be served, then we will remain starving for the One Who is truth, Who came not to be served, but to serve.

Brothers and sisters, where is the saintly fire of old? Where is our humility, our love, our prayer for mercy? I will not accuse anyone here except for myself. I have much work to do. I have been waiting for this holy season of Lent which is now coming soon, and I have been praying that my own eyes and my heart may be opened for what God would do within me, so that I, too, may find mercy, so that I, too, may ask how I can preach this Gospel which is given to me not for my own possession but rather so that it may be multiplied all around me.

So we begin this great quest for this year, the search for the meaning of our Lenten labors. This year, let it begin with the humility of the Publican, who asks for forgiveness and mercy so that he can be set back into a right relationship with God and with those whom he has cheated.

If we make our journey toward Pascha in humility, then it will be a journey of evangelism, a journey of service, a journey of giving that good word of Jesus Christ to those around us. It is not only to invite the stranger to church, but most especially to begin by inviting those next to us—whether they once shared this space with us and are no longer here, whether they only share this space with us every so often, or whether they have not yet come here into this holy place.

For everyone we know belongs here. Everyone is properly a member of this church. No one is shut out. No one is excluded. No one has a priority. We are all called.

Who will listen? Who will come? Who will fall down before God and cry out with the Publican, "God, be merciful to me, a sinner"? Who today will make it their mission this Lent to restore those who have been lost to us, to bring closer to us those whose connection is only tenuous, and to bring into our midst those who belong to us but have not yet become one with God in the flesh?

Let our Lenten evangelism begin. And let it begin with humility.

To God therefore be all glory, honor and worship, to the Father and to the Son and to the Holy Spirit, now and ever, and unto ages of ages. Amen.

Appendix F
Entry #19
Forgiveness

"A New Series On Forgiveness" May 7, 2015.

For the next 30 days I will write a daily post on forgiveness. I have gathered ideas and methods to prepare for International Forgiveness Day on August 2nd, but because forgiveness is a process I thought we would start now. There is usually someone in our life who needs forgiveness from us. I hope I am able to show "forgiveness is not an occasional act, it is a constant attitude" Martin Luther King, Jr.

There are more people out there than we realize who at some point find forgiveness difficult. The difficulty, or impossibility to some, usually involves one or two people or a certain type of offense. The next 30 days are designed to help the person who finds forgiveness difficult by providing practical, common sense steps.

The last thing I would like to say is how pleasurable this should be. Sometimes the right thing to do is hard and unpleasant, but forgiveness is neither. If we embrace the attitude Martin Luther King, Jr. suggests, it can be both pleasant and easier than holding a grudge. If hate creates a burden and stress, then love lifts us up and relieves the stress. Only love can dispel hate. Only kindness can overcome cruelty. Only compassion can melt indifference.

Question: Are you struggling with forgiveness right now?

"Forgiveness Day 1: Science Proves Forgiveness Is For Everyone, Not Just Religious People" May 8th, 2015. In 1985 the only people who talked about forgiveness were doing it in some way related to a religious teaching. Dr. Robert Enright, a psychology professor at the University of Wisconsin, sought to change that. He began clinical research on forgiveness and established the International Forgiveness Institute in 1994. He wanted to prove that forgiveness was beneficial on an anatomical and physiological level. Dr. Enright "created the first scientifically proven forgiveness program in the country" (http://internationalforgiveness.com/about-us.htm).

His revolutionary work showed that forgiveness can be a development of capabilities, like reasoning. From that he developed a 20 step process of forgiveness. The process can be found in the book *Forgiveness Is A Choice*, published by the American Psychological Association.

Here is the good news. Whether you are a Christian, Buddhist, Atheist, or Agnostic, there is scientific evidence that forgiveness is critical to your well being.

Question: Did you know forgiveness was not limited to religious people?

"Forgiveness Day 2: The Definition Is Key" May 9th, 2015. The first and most important thing when learning forgiveness is to define the term. Most problems with forgiveness comes from misunderstanding the word or confusing it with other words. To keep clear, we will reference several different definitions to help give you the full concept.

One of my favorite definitions from Psychologist Sonja Lyubomirsky. She calls forgiveness a shift in thinking towards the other person. Here are the definition of "forgive" from dictionary.com:
1. to grant pardon for or remission of (an offense, debt, etc.); absolve.
2. to give up all claim on account of; remit (a debt, obligation, etc.).
3. to grant pardon to (a person).
4. to cease to feel resentment against: *to forgive one's enemies.*
5. to cancel an indebtedness or liability of: *to forgive the interest owed on a loan.*

Synonyms include: See excuse, absolve, or acquit. It is not surprising we are having difficulty with forgiveness after reading through those five definitions, or even seeing the synonym "excuse" up there. The leading psychologist in the field of forgiveness have focused on giving us better understanding of the word. Much of their research is focused on helping the world understand that forgiveness is not.

Forgiveness is not:
1. **excusing: demeans the offense**
2. **condoning: is ignoring the problem**
3. **trusting: is about the future, not the past**
4. **reconciliation: is about trust**
5. **justice: is not relinquished when you forgive**
6. **revenge: is when you take justice into your own hands**

Unfortunately dictionary.com kept their best definition of forgiveness at the bottom of the page. It reads, "The modern sense of "to give up desire or power to punish." When I traveled over to Merriam-Webster I found what I was looking for:
- to stop feeling anger toward (someone who has done something wrong) : to stop blaming (someone)
- to stop feeling anger about (something) : to forgive someone for (something wrong)
- to stop requiring payment of (money that is owed)

The key word above is "feeling". Feelings can control us, make us trapped. Anger is a trap, as well as disappointment, depression, and a sense of martyrdom. To forgive is to change how we feel about something so that we are no longer controlled by negative feelings.

Question: Were you confusing forgiveness with other words?

"Forgiveness Day 10: Are You In The Dark" May 18, 2015. There have been too many stories of miners trapped in a collapsed cave. One of the long term dangers of being trapped in a cave is permanent blindness. The human eyeball can become permanently blind if in complete darkness for two weeks or more.

Remember the pain when coming out of a dark movie theatre on a bright day. That was only two hours of darkness while staring at a bright movie screen. Imagine the pain from coming out of several days of total darkness.

Without stimulation the eyeball stops trying to see. When our resentment stays in the dark, over time we stop trying to let go of the hurt. Shedding light may have an initial increase in pain, but as the pain subsides we are able to see.

With light comes not only the ability to see but also clarity, awareness, and warmth. With darkness comes only a cold denial of reality. Shine some light on the darkness inside. It may hurt a bit, but that pain is necessary for healing.

Question: Are you ready to pursue the warm light of forgiveness?

Appendix G
Entry #24
Liturgical Language

"Why Americans Need An All-English Liturgy" *by Robert Arakaki, taken from www.orthodoxbridge.com*

In 2007, *Christianity Today* published an article, "Will the Twenty First Century be the Orthodox Century?" In it Bradley Nassif argued that Orthodoxy will indeed grow and expand in this coming century. But in an *Again Magazine* article, "The Orthodox Christian Opportunity," Nassif noted although many people are converting to Orthodoxy, significant numbers of these converts are also leaving through the backdoor discouraged and disenchanted. Much of the reasons for their disenchantment lie not with the Orthodox Faith *per se*, but with the realities of Orthodox parishes. Nassif refers to this problem as Orthodoxy's backdoor.

One of the major obstacles to the twenty first century becoming the Orthodox century is the language barrier. In many American Orthodox parishes the Sunday Liturgy is either in a foreign language or a mixture of English and non-English. Orthodox parishes with an all-English Liturgy tend to be in the minority. This blog posting addresses why we need all-English worship services, what can be done about the present problem of people exiting through the backdoor, and how we can help make the twenty first century the Orthodox century.

The Liturgy as the Front Door

The Liturgy is Orthodoxy's front door. It is often the first place where people encounter Orthodoxy. There they see Orthodoxy in action: people worshiping the Holy Trinity. The Liturgy is also essential for becoming Orthodox. One cannot become Orthodox just by reading Orthodox books or visiting Orthodox blogs, one becomes Orthodox through participation in the right worship of the Holy Trinity.

However, people sometimes find Orthodoxy's front door blocked when they attend a worship service where the Liturgy is done in a foreign language. Many visitors walk out after hearing nothing but Greek for the first few minutes of the Liturgy. It can be a painful experience. Many feel excluded, bewildered, and lost.

Linguistic zigzags — where the priest prays in English and the choir responds in non-English — are not uncommon in many ethnic parishes. For the unwary worshiper, it is like driving along on a smooth asphalt road then all of a sudden hitting a pothole. This can lead to a jarring, frustrating, and tiring worship experience. What should be a meaningful worship encounter with God becomes more like a tutorial in Greek, Slavonic, Serbian, Arabic, etc. Even several years after becoming Orthodox, many converts find themselves struggling with the Liturgy in a foreign language. People lose their place in the order of the Liturgy. It is not realistic to expect all converts to adjust to the Liturgy not being completely in English; some can make the adjustment, but many cannot. Continuous exposure to the Liturgy in a foreign language does not necessarily make it easier over time. As a result converts often find the Liturgy more a burden than a delight. And so converts are becoming frustrated and some are dropping out. These are not conditions conducive for spiritual growth.

Worship in the vernacular is the long-standing Tradition of Orthodoxy. This liturgical principle is rooted in the miracle of Pentecost. On that day the Christians spoke in tongues to a international gathering who were astonished to

"hear them declaring the wonders of God in *our own tongues*!" (Acts 2:11, NIV, italics added)

The Apostle Paul emphasized the importance of worship engaging our understanding. He wrote:

"But in the church I would rather speak five *intelligible words* to instruct others than ten thousand words in a tongue." (I Corinthians 14:19, NIV)

Orthodox Missionary Practice

The history of Orthodox missions is full of examples of the use of the vernacular. A prominent example is Saints Kyril and Methodios translating the Liturgy into Slavonic. Another example is Saint Nicholas of Japan laboring many years to master the Japanese language before translating the Liturgy into Japanese. A third example is Saint Innocent of Alaska who translated the Gospels into the Aleut language. Non-vernacular worship — so widespread in America — represents a departure from historic Orthodoxy. Thus, it is an *innovation inconsistent with Holy Tradition*. This innovation arose more from circumstance than deliberate choice. What was the vernacular for the first generation immigrants later became an incomprehensible language for the second and third generations, and for converts from another ethnic background. An innovation that arose from inaction requires deliberate action to bring the church back into conformity with Tradition.

Let Us Be Attentive!

The word "liturgy" means "the work of the people." But the people can't do their job of worshiping God effectively if the language is not their own. We are called to love God with all our mind (Mark 12:30) but worship in a foreign language gets in the way of our being able to worship God intelligently. Rather than assisting in worship, the non-vernacular hinders us.

One reason why the Liturgy should be entirely in English is Orthodoxy expects its members to be fully attentive in their worship. On several occasions during the Liturgy, the priest will call out: "Let us be attentive!" But if peoples' minds start to drift when the priest switches to Greek (or some other foreign language), they are not really being attentive to the Liturgy. The problem is not with the worshiper, but the fact most people find it difficult to worship in an unfamiliar language.

Another reason for an all-English Liturgy is the Apostle Paul's insistence that worship be in a language understandable to the listener. He wrote:

"Unless you speak intelligible words with your tongue, how will anyone know what you are saying? You will just be speaking into the air." (I Corinthians 14:9, NIV)

The danger here is that the Liturgy will turn into empty worship — something that the Old Testament prophets and Jesus denounced in no uncertain terms:

"These people come near to me with their mouth and honor me with their lips, but their hearts are far from me." (Isaiah 29:13; Matthew 15:8-9, NIV)

The Liturgy as Catechism

The Liturgy constitutes an ongoing catechism for Orthodox Christians. It continually reminds us of the fundamental doctrines of Orthodoxy. When understood, the Liturgy has a profound impact on our faith and worship. But, is not the Liturgy's power to shape our thinking weakened by it being sung in an incomprehensible tongue? A danger of non-vernacular worship is parishioners can become so focused on phonetically reproducing the Liturgy they barely pay attention to the great truths being proclaimed in the Liturgy. If it is shrouded in language that is not comprehended, then the Liturgy will become an ethnic rite having little power to challenge us to live holy lives for God.

I visited a number of Orthodox services while I was at Gordon-Conwell Theological Seminary, but they were mostly in Greek. It was not until I came to Berkeley and attended the all-English Liturgy at Saints Kyril and Methodios

Bulgarian Orthodox Church that I was able to connect with the Liturgy and that the Liturgy began to reshape my theology and spirituality. It was the two years of hearing the Liturgy there that laid the foundation for my becoming Orthodox.

In addition to teaching us what the Church believes, the Liturgy also protects us from heresy. However, if the Liturgy is sung in a language poorly understood, its catechetical function is compromised. A priest once discovered a parishioner did not really believe in the perpetual virginity of Mary. He pointed to one of the antiphons which is sung every Sunday, "Only Begotten" (Monogenes), which affirms Mary's perpetual virginity. However, the parishioner never got the point because in that parish the antiphon was normally sung in Greek, not in English. In the long run, a non-comprehended Liturgy makes Orthodoxy vulnerable to heterodoxy and nominalism among the laity, not to mention people dropping out of the Church altogether. Orthodox laity whose grasp of Orthodox doctrine is weak or hazy will not be able to defend their Orthodox beliefs, nor will they be able to effectively live out their Orthodox convictions.

Ethnic Parishes

Many Orthodox parishes in America today are what can be considered ethnic parishes. They were founded by immigrants and continue to be under the care of hierarchs in the old country. The ethnic parish preserves the old country's culture through the following means: (1) the language used in the Sunday Liturgy, (2) the food served on special occasions, (3) ethnic festivals and holidays, and (4) language classes. Ethnic parishes tend to diligently celebrate the lives of their ethnic saints while hardly making mention of American Orthodox saints.

<u>Metropolitan Philip</u> of the Antiochian Orthodox Christian Archdiocese observed:

We consider ourselves Americans, and we are proud of it-except when we go to church, we suddenly become Greeks, Russians, Arabs, and Albanians.

(Again Magazine *vol. 28 no. 2, p.5)*

Ethnic parishes are an important part of Orthodoxy in America. It is in large part because of Orthodox immigrants who founded Orthodox parishes that Orthodoxy has such a widespread presence in American society today. Yet it is not realistic to expect that ethnic parishes are capable of evangelizing America. Orthodoxy is growing in America, but much of this growth is due to the planting of Orthodox parishes with all-English Liturgies. Ethnic parishes are not built that way; they are primarily suited to preserving the language, customs, and holidays of the old country. As such, they are designed for the first generation immigrants and their descendants, but not for American converts.

The term "old country" is not a pejorative term (as some might think) but a term accepted and used by social scientists, especially in the emergent field of postcolonial studies. Robin Cohen in *Global Diasporas: An Introduction* described "diasporic communities" as a community who live in one country while acknowledging that the "old country" has some claim on their loyalty and emotions (p. ix) and exerts a powerful influence on their social identity. Ties between the diasporic community and the "old country" can be especially intense in cases like the Greek-American community. In the *Report to His Eminence ARCHBISHOP IAKOVOS* (1990) it was noted that Greek-Americans are understood to be viewed either as **an extension of the Greek homeland** (*homogenia*) or as entrants and then participants in American history (p. 22; emphasis added).

Ethnic identity becomes even more complicated and fraught when a diasporic community shares the same social space, e.g., a local church, with Americans for whom the US is the only homeland they know of. This is what happens when an ethnic parish finds a growing presence of mainstream Americans joining them. They are confused that people would want to join the parish just because they want to be Orthodox. Many Americans want to become Orthodox, but very few want to assimilate into an ethnic parish and learn a foreign language and abide by foreign customs of the old country. To compel others to assimilate into a culture is contrary to the Orthodox tradition of missions and can even lead to cultural imperialism.

Jesus' parable of the need to pour new wine into new wineskins and the foolishness of pouring new wine into old wineskins (Mark 2:22) applies to the present situation. Ethnic parishes are not well suited to meet the needs of converts from the outside. They can handle small numbers of converts, but if the numbers of converts become more than a trickle then the ethnic core can start to feel threatened resulting in a backlash. They will fear that the new members will undermine the ethnic identity of their parish, especially if the newcomers want more English in the Sunday worship.

There is no question that people have come to Orthodoxy via ethnic parishes, but their numbers are such that the long term impact will be minimal. If America is to embrace Orthodoxy, this trickle of converts will need to become a broad stream of converts. Ethnic parishes throw an unnecessary hurdle for non-ethnic for the above reasons. When it comes to evangelism ethnic parishes are like the eagle which is well suited for soaring in the sky, but unlike the duck is not well suited for life along the lake. In short, ethnic parishes are not set up for effective evangelism.

If Orthodoxy is to effectively evangelize America, an all-English Liturgy is essential. Orthodoxy's future in America depends on the availability of an all-English Liturgy to ordinary Americans. The vast majority of Americans are monolingual English speakers. They are not comfortable with worshiping in a foreign language; nor will they be interested in shedding their American identity at the church entrance on Sunday morning. See my article on the three waves of Orthodoxy in America.

Changing Ethnic Parishes?

Can ethnic parishes be moved towards all-English liturgies? For the most part, I don't think so. I've heard priests tell me they are gradually moving towards more English in the Liturgy, but what I have seen has been more of a back and forth movement in which very little change is made in the long run. Many parish priests are caught in a difficult situation of holding together a diverse parish community. While they personally may favor an all-English Liturgy, they also need to accommodate the needs and concerns of the longtime members (many of whom contribute substantially to the priest's salary). It is a good idea to tell your parish priest you want an all-English Liturgy, but my advice is not to expect much to happen. Furthermore, it should be kept in mind that ultimately it is the bishop who has the final say over the language used in the parish's Sunday worship.

There are Orthodox hierarchs who have called for the

"preservation and promotion of our Hellenic ethos and tradition."

Thus, ethnic Orthodox parishes are more than the result of circumstances, rather they have their roots in the priorities and policies of both local parishes and the hierarchy. Those of us who desire all-English Liturgies need to respect their understanding of Orthodox missions and work actively with Orthodox jurisdictions that support all-English Liturgies and the evangelization of America.

Pan-Orthodox Parishes?

Pan-Orthodox parishes represent a different kind of missions strategy. Where there is not a large enough immigrant community to form an ethnic parish, one finds various ethnic groups cobbled together to form a single parish. In these parishes one can find the Lord's Prayer in Greek, Slavonic, Serbian, Arabic, as well as English. The underlying premise of pan-Orthodox parishes seems to be that we should all hold on to the culture and languages of the old country, even though we're all Americans, and our children are Americans, and most of us have no intention of moving back to the old country. The problem with pan-

Orthodox parishes is they hold little appeal for many Americans. Pan-Orthodox parishes resemble the synthetic culture of the United Nations than real cultures that people inhabit. Because the culture of pan-Orthodox parishes are alien to mainstream American society, they are not capable of effective evangelism.

Pan-Orthodox parishes are like ethnic parishes in their retrospective focus on the old country. They therefore share all the problems mentioned above in regards to ethnic parishes. People without doubt will join these parishes but in the long run such parishes will exert only a minimal influence on the city or area they live in.

Dual Track Strategy

If we are to bring America to Orthodoxy then we need a dual-track approach. We need Orthodox parishes with all-English worship services, **and** we need ethnic Orthodox parishes whose ethos and language reflects that of the old country.

The dual track strategy is as old as the book of Acts. In the beginning of Acts, we read how multitudes of people converted to Christianity. But what is often overlooked is the fact that this movement was taking place among the Hebrew speaking Jews of Palestine. When we come to the sixth chapter, tension was growing between the Hebrew speaking Jews and the Greek speaking Jews. Communication difficulties led to many Greek speaking widows being overlooked in the daily distribution of food. Unlike the Jews who were fluent in Hebrew, the Hellenistic Jews' mother tongue was Greek. The root of the problem lay not in sinful attitudes, but in honest linguistic and cultural differences. The problem was resolved by the creation of a dual track or bicultural leadership structure. The Apostles who were ethnically Palestinian Jews appointed Greek speaking Jews to the diaconate. This is evident by the prevalence of non-Jewish names: Stephen, Philip, Procorus, Nicanor, Timon, and Parmenas (Acts 6:5). Also noteworthy is the fact that one of them, Nicolas, was a Gentile who converted to Judaism. The result was that

"the number of disciples in Jerusalem increased rapidly." (Acts 6:7)

Precedence for the dual track strategy can be found in the Antiochian Archdiocese allowing for both the Byzantine rite and the Western rite. A parish can elect to use one or the other but not both. This policy makes much sense and is practical. It also gives a parish liturgical stability. I would suggest that each parish be given the option of worshiping either in English or in the language of the old country, but not both. As noted earlier, mixed language worship is an innovation that has no precedence in the history of Orthodoxy.

Orthodoxy can learn something from the experience of the Japanese American churches. They encouraged their children to learn English, and they gave strong support for English services. Where the older *isseis* (first generation) worshiped in Japanese, the younger *nisseis* (second generation) and *sanseis* (third generation) met in a separate service to worship in English. In other words, what looked from the outside like a single parish, was in actuality a dual-track parish. This missions strategy allowed the Japanese American churches to preserve church unity in the face of inter generational differences and avoid large numbers of youths dropping out for lack of interest.

Under the dual track strategy, the parish will have a main sanctuary for the English-speaking congregation and a side chapel for the ethnic congregation. This is needed to follow the rubric that only one Eucharist be celebrated per day. This means that a dual-track Orthodox parish will need to have at least two priests assigned to the parish to celebrate the Eucharist. This calls for a deliberate long-term missions strategy fully supported by the bishop of that city. If successful, we will see a network of dozens Orthodox parishes in each major city. Some parishes will worship in the language of the old country, but the majority of the parishes will worship in English. In this twenty first century diocese, Orthodoxy's ethnic diversity is affirmed without any blurring of ethnic identity. This arrangement will reflect not just America's growing cultural diversity, but also the catholicity of the Orthodox Church.

People might object that liturgical rubrics call for only one Eucharist to be celebrated in a parish per day and that the dual-track strategy being proposed is contrary to the established rubrics. My response is that what is being called for is an *oikonomia* or pastoral dispensation in light of unusual circumstances. It should be noted that we already have a de facto *oikonomia* given the widespread tolerance of two violations of Orthodox canon law:

(1) multiple bishops in the same city, and

(2) the widespread usage of non-vernacular in the Liturgy.

The dual track strategy should be seen as an *oikonomia,* a temporary measure, until we have an American Orthodox Church. What is presented here is more of a suggestion to get a discussion going. The Orthodox community, both laity and clergy, need to have an open and frank discussion about how Orthodoxy can deal with the serious problem of the non-vernacular Liturgy.

Antiochian Breakthrough

In <u>The Bridges of God</u>, Donald McGavran, former professor of missions at Fuller Seminary, observe there are two approaches to missions: the mission station approach and the people movement approach. The mission station approach tends to be static with the mission station serving as the religious and cultural center for a group of expatriates and their converts. The people movement approach is dynamic with multitudes becoming Christians. The difference lies in their long term focus. Where the mission station is content with establishing a beachhead presence in a country, the people movement approach seeks to move inland to where the vast majority live. Orthodoxy today is situated in an awkward in-between situation. Thanks to the immigrants who founded ethnic parishes, Orthodoxy has a beachhead presence in every major American city. At the same time, Orthodoxy has barely moved inland where the vast majority live.

In the book of Acts we see the tension between the mission station approach and the people movement approach. In the opening chapters of Acts we read how thousands accepted Jesus as the Messiah. The early Christian movement was largely Jewish in makeup and centered in Jerusalem. This is characteristic of the mission station approach. Although we read of Gentiles becoming Christians in the early chapters of Acts (e.g., the Ethiopian eunuch and Cornelius the Centurion), these conversions represent little pockets of converts that lay on the margins of their culture. Christianity did not become a broad people movement until the Antiochian breakthrough.

Now those who had been scattered by the persecution in connection with Stephen traveled as far as Phoenicia, Cyprus and Antioch, telling the message **only to Jews.** Some of them, however, men from Cyprus and Cyrene, went to Antioch and began to speak **to Greeks also**, telling them the good news about the Lord Jesus. The Lord's hand was with them, and a great number of people believed and turned to the Lord. (Acts 11:19-21, NIV; bold added)

What is notable about this passage is that some spoke "only to the Jews." Although the persecution dispersed Christians geographically, much of the communication of the Gospel flowed within the confines of Jewish culture. It was not until Antioch that some spoke the Christian message "to Greeks also," that is, to the non-Jews that the long standing cultural barrier was breached; Christianity became a broad multicultural movement and the evangelization of the Roman Empire began in earnest.

Opening the Door to the Future

Business as usual cannot continue. Orthodoxy in America needs to restructure and retool itself if we are to effectively evangelize American society. One important (if not essential) way of retooling is to encourage and support all-English Orthodox services across America. If we have the Liturgy in English, people will come and they will stay. There is a growing spiritual hunger in America, and we can help these spiritually hungry people discover Jesus Christ who is the Way, the Truth, and Life. By committing ourselves to all-English services, Orthodoxy will be opening the front door and closing the back door.

Having an Antiochian breakthrough in twenty first century American society will require brave men and women who will sacrificially commit themselves to starting Orthodox missions in areas where there are no Orthodox parishes or where there are language barriers. The aim here is to have all-English Orthodox parishes across the country within reasonable driving distance. Two particular jurisdictions have been notable for their willingness to engage in starting up new missions:

- the Antiochian Orthodox Christian Archdiocese, and
- the Orthodox Church in America.

Interested readers are encouraged to contact these offices and inquire about opportunities for starting up an all-English Orthodox parish in their area.

It is also important that we not seek to change ethnic parishes. Attempting to do so is likely to be met with stiff resistance, while wasting precious time and energies. Rather than complain about the difficulties of non-English services, the better approach is to have a positive attitude and to take positive steps like helping to start all-English Orthodox missions. It is also important that mainstream Americans be supportive of ethnic Orthodox who wish to affirm their ethnic heritage. Ethnic Orthodox Christians have a rich cultural heritage that has been shaped by the Orthodox ethos over many generations. This is something many modern Americans lack. I once asked an Orthodox friend how he understood his ethnic heritage, all he could say was that he was a "mutt" — a hybrid of Scot, Irish, English, German and what have you — and that his ethnicity is "American." We need to regard each other with respect and charity.

Twelve Reasons

Here are twelve reasons Orthodoxy in America need an all-English Liturgy:

- Liturgy in the vernacular is part of Holy Tradition;
- Scripture teaches the importance of intelligible worship (Acts 2:11, I Corinthians 14:19);
- Scripture teaches the priority of loving God with our mind (Mark 12:30);
- The Liturgy means "the work of the people" and the use of incomprehensible non-vernacular languages hinders people from doing their work of worshiping God;
- The use of the non-vernacular impairs the Liturgy's function of educating worshipers in fundamental Orthodox doctrines;

- The use of non-English met the needs of the first generation immigrants but is ill-suited for the needs of second and third generations, and mainstream Americans;
- Compromise solutions like pan-Orthodox parishes have in many instances failed to work;
- The use of the non-vernacular have caused visitors to walk out;
- The use of the non-vernacular have frustrated converts and caused some to become discouraged and drop out of church life;
- The use of the non-vernacular combined with a parish identity centered around a particular ethnicity have caused many converts to feel like outsiders;
- The use of the non-vernacular is contrary to Orthodox missionary practice; and
- The use of the non-vernacular is a major impediment to the evangelization of American society.

Orthodoxy in 2100?

As we stand at the start of the twenty first century, we need to ask ourselves what our vision is for Orthodoxy in America. If we maintain the present course, what will Orthodoxy in America look like in the year 2100? Will there be the same small number of ethnic Orthodox parishes (maybe a little bigger) or will there be dozens of Orthodox parishes all over our city and people coming to Orthodoxy by droves? This is beginning to happen. The May 2007 edition of *The Word* reported that twenty-five catechumens were received into the Orthodox Church at St. Barnabas, Costa Mesa, CA. If we pass up this challenge, American Orthodoxy could end up an obscure religious curiosity.

The present interest in Orthodoxy represents both an opportunity and a challenge for Orthodox laity, clergy, and hierarchy. If we rise up to the challenge, we can expect to see unprecedented growth and vitality for American Orthodoxy, and the twenty first century will be on its way to becoming the Orthodox century.

Appendix H
Entry #43
Acolyte Training

- When the acolyte enters the altar area he immediately does three metanias facing the altar.
- Then approach the lead priest for a blessing.
    - Say "Father bless." The priest will bless your vestment, kiss his hand quickly. Say "Amen" when the priest is finished.
- The acolyte then goes to into one of the side rooms to vest and says this prayer as he is vesting.
    - I will come into thy house in the multitude of thy mercy; and in thy fear I will worship toward thy holy temple. My soul shall be joyful in the Lord; for He hath clothed me with the garment of salvation; and the robe of gladness He has wrapped around me. He has placed on me, as a bridegroom, a crown; He has adorned me, as a bride, with jewels.
- Captains, those 13 and older, will pick their side and their junior acolyte.
- When lining up for the Little Entrance, stand opposite of your side. This will keep you from having to switch out on the ambo when you separate to come in.
- After you come in from the Little Entrance, the lanterns will stand on the north and south sides of the altar, and the junior acolytes will stand next to each other 5 ft beyond the altar facing the altar (west).
- For the Great Entrance, line up as soon as the deacon stops speaking and face the altar. There is a line in the cement directly in the large door way across from the altar (same line as before), line up there facing the altar (west).
    - Order: small cross, lantern, fan, cross, fan, lantern, small cross
    - As soon as the priest goes out to cense, the cross and lanterns will move to the north door and the fans stand by in the corner.
- The Great Entrance is the only time you will all file in together. All other times separate and come through the door on your side.
- After filing in from the Great Entrance line up facing east, all bow together, then put processional items away. You do not have to wait for the priest to cense to line up and put items away. We only did this in the old church because of space.

Acolyte Hand Signals

 Open the door

 Light the lantern

 Light the candle

 Light the coal

 Put incense in censor

 Give censor to clergy

 Holy Bread to Father, remove napkins

 Carry the big Cross

 Carry the little Cross

 Carry a fan

 Carry a lantern

 Carry a candle

 Line up

 Heat water/ take to clergy

Appendix I
Entry #45
Becoming Truly Human

"An Invitation to Become Truly Human" *by Charles Ajalat, Fr. George Kevorkian, Fr. Michael Nasser, and Sub-deacon Adam Roberts.*

Our lives in this modern world become so busy that we are constantly distracted from asking ourselves the fundamental questions and reflecting on the importance of their meaning in our lives. As Fr. Thomas Hopko of blessed memory said in The Lenten Spring,

> People feel unhappy and they don't know why. They feel that something is wrong, but they can't put their finger on what.... They have everything, yet they want more. And when they get more, they are still left ... dissatisfied. They want happiness and peace, but nothing seems to bring it. They want fulfillment, but it never seems to come. Everything is fine, and yet everything is wrong.... It is covered over by frantic activity, and endless running around.... It is drowned out by television programs and video games. But when the movement stops, and the power is turned off, and everything is quiet ... then the dread sets in, and the meaninglessness of it all and the boredom and the fear. Why is this so? Because the Church tells us that we are really not at home. We are alienated and estranged from our true country. We are not with God in the land of the living. We are spiritually sick, and some of us are already dead [spiritually].

There are perhaps 60 million unchurched people in America who have not been to a church in six months. Perhaps one-half of these are individuals who previously attended a church earlier in their lives. Almost all of the "unchurched," however, have not been exposed to the understanding of God in the Orthodox Church, which has preserved the apostolic doctrine handed to the Apostles from Christ Himself. While our Archdiocesan churches have always been open to those who found their way to us, few of our parishes have undertaken efforts to seek out those around us who hunger and thirst for the Orthodox Faith, whether they realize their hunger or not.

Under the leadership of Metropolitan Joseph, who wants our neighbors to have the opportunity to receive the blessings of Orthodoxy that we enjoy, our Archdiocese is making a new effort to that end. The idea originated in 2009, when Charles Ajalat spoke out for the need of the Church to be the Church by following our Lord's Great Commission: "Go, therefore, and make disciples of all the nations ... teaching them to observe all things that I have commanded you ..." (Matthew 28:19–20). The laity must, under the guidance of the priest, also take this commandment to heart. St. John Chrysostom says it emphatically: "I do not believe in the salvation of anyone who does not try to save others." As Fr. Peter Gillquist of blessed memory said, too: "You don't have to be a gifted evangelist to take part in being an effective witness for Christ."

The "Becoming Truly Human" program offers those outside the Church a comfortable, inviting and gentle introduction to the fullness of our human lives, as offered within Orthodox Christianity. The goal of the program is to help fulfill the Great Commission according to the two Great Commandments of Christ: Love the Lord your God with all your heart and all your mind and all your soul, and love your neighbor as yourself.

Why is the course called, "Becoming Truly Human"? Aren't we "human" now? The answer is No. We need to understand what it means to be truly a human being, made in the image of God, and to understand that the purpose of life is to have an intimate relationship with God through His Church. St. Ignatius of Antioch, on his journey to his martyrdom, begged his followers not to prevent his death, because to die and be with Christ is to live, to be truly human. It is because God created us so: "Let us make the human being in our image, after our likeness" (Genesis 1:26). Nicholas Cabasilas said, "To sum it up: the Savior first and alone showed to us the true human being, who is perfect on account of both character and life and in all other respects." St. Athanasius has said that only through Christ's death and resurrection and our resulting re-creation, can man "become truly human." Fr. John Behr, Dean of St. Vladimir's Seminary, has suggested in his speeches and work on death, that perhaps only in death are we ultimately truly human, for then we see fully the reality of God and His Kingdom.

The program runs once a week for eight weeks, including a one- or two-day retreat. There is an on-site four-hour training session for those who will be administering and helping. The course is designed not to be a burden on the parish priest, but led by local church leaders who are trusted and approved by the priest. This is a real opportunity for the priest to empower the laity while furthering the work of the Church.

The way the course is run for newcomers is based on the researched premise that people become Christians because someone they know and admire is a Christian and they want to know, therefore, what Christianity is really all about. The setting for the dinner and course is a home or inviting church hall (perhaps with candle light and a warm atmosphere) or other suitable setting. Each session of the program starts with an informal dinner, followed by a twenty-minute talk from someone speaking extemporaneously, but conveying material from a script that is provided. (Alternatively, we hope to have professionally produced twenty-minute videos available later).

The eight session topics include fundamental questions, such as, What is the purpose of life? Who is Jesus? Why did He die? and How can I have faith? After the talk there are discussion groups. Each group has a moderator, who does not have to be theologically trained, but whose role simply is to keep the discussion going and not let any one person dominate.

The program ideas were developed in 2014 by a committee co-chaired by former Chancellor Charles Ajalat and the Metropolitan's assistant, Fr. George Kevorkian. Bishop Nicholas served as the episcopal overseer. Fr. Ken DeVoie of the Missions and Evangelism Department wrote the first draft of the materials. The program was then transferred from the Department to be directly under the Metropolitan. It was funded for the first two years by the Orthodox Vision Foundation and the Archdiocese. Although initiated in the Archdiocese, the hope is that, after an experimental and refining stage, the program will spread to all Orthodox jurisdictions in this country and elsewhere.

"Becoming Truly Human" is a vehicle to share the Orthodox Christian view of life with others, while revitalizing the faith of parishioners. The "Becoming Truly Human" course is not a catechetical course, but an evangelistic one. The ultimate goal is that many of the newcomers taking the course may go on to an inquirer's course or catechetical course under the priest. Thus they may begin the transformation of their own lives, becoming committed chrismated or baptized Orthodox Christians.

The course is now being given experimentally in 14 Antiochian parishes, with another 27-plus planning on beginning the course between now and the end of September. These over 40 churches include large parishes, small parishes and missions, "cradle" and "convert" parishes, churches in each diocese and churches (so far) from 23 states and provinces.

All of the courses, except one, are in Phase 1 – the running of the course among existing parishioners internally in the parish so that they might not only be revitalized themselves, but feel comfortable inviting friends, business acquaintances and unchurched family members to Phase 2. So far, the courses generally have been enthusiastically received. One church, having finished Phase 1, has started Phase 2 with college students. This version of the course is for those from beyond the parish who might be interested in exploring Christianity. After that group's first session, all the comments were positive. One person stated, "There aren't many places I've been where I could be involved in a discussion like this." His comment points to the problems – the lack of a forum to discuss the important questions of life, and fear of "organized religion" – and it shows the need for a solution like the "Becoming Truly Human" program, presented in a warm, friendly, loving environment.

The Patriarchs of the Orthodox Church jointly said in 2008, "The evangelization of God's people, and also of those who don't believe in Christ, constitutes the supreme duty of the Church." Patriarch Ignatius said on February 6, 1987, "The Orthodox Church is not only for one nation, one civilization, one continent. It is like God Himself, for all and for every place." His successor, Patriarch John X, made clear that evangelism or spiritual outreach is our task in this Archdiocese, and our tradition in Antioch, where they were first called Christians (Acts 11:26): "In this beloved Archdiocese, evangelism realizes a full sense of the historic missionary vocation of Antioch." Metropolitan Joseph, at his enthronement, said emphatically, "I shall use this staff to proclaim the Gospel [the good news]."

But what is that "good news?" The "good news," Fr. Keiser writes in *Spread the Word*, "is that Jesus came to establish the Kingdom of God." If we do not start understanding and living in the Kingdom of God now during our lifetimes, uniting both our faith and our actions, our souls may well not live in the Kingdom of God at the time of our death, when our souls leave our bodies until soul and body are reunited in the general resurrection.

How are we, as an Archdiocese, doing in fulfilling the mission of the Church in bringing the Gospel, as understood by the historic Church, to the more than sixty million unchurched in America? Unfortunately, not as well as we should be. According to the Archdiocese census information, as the best available measure of newcomers, 88 percent of our more than 275 churches and missions have four or fewer chrismations per year. There is no reason, however, why all of the top twenty churches (in terms of chrismations), if not all our churches, cannot each have thirty chrismations per year. Although increases in chrismations and baptisms of the unbaptized likely will be slower in the beginning, if God blesses the implementation of the "Becoming Truly Human" program, in 16 years the Archdiocese could double the number of its faithful. Equally, if not more importantly, if God blesses the program there will be a change in culture, so that all of the Archdiocese's churches will be interested in evangelism or spiritual outreach, and there will be a desire on the part of all in the churches that they be warm and welcoming places for those who want to know Christ's Church.

How can you be involved in the "Becoming Truly Human" program? 1. Pray for those administering and participating in the program; 2. Help start the program in your own parish; and 3. Donate to the "Becoming Truly Human" Evangelism Fund, by sending a check so marked, to the Antiochian Archdiocese, 358 Mountain Road, Englewood, NJ 07631. Your generous gift will help insure that the program, as blessed by God, may produce bountiful fruit. Beyond the need for resources as the program expands among the parishes, there is a need for a website, for the production and sale of materials and videos for the program, and much more.

How can your parish be involved in the "Becoming Truly Human" program? If you have the blessings of your priest, and together with him can find a potential local administrator for the program, contact the program director, Adam Roberts, **adamr@antiochian.org** (615-971-0000), or the program's consultant, Fr. Michael Nasser, **frmichaeln@gmail.com** (270-823-3371).

Pray that the "Becoming Truly Human" program will revitalize many of the faithful and accomplish God's will by bringing many additional new, wonderful, committed Orthodox Christians, whether originally "cradle" or converts, into His Church, so that they might have a foretaste now, and live forever, in the Kingdom of God.

"Go, therefore, and make disciples of all the nations ... teaching them to observe all things that I have commanded you ..." (Matthew 28:19–20).

From The Word, *June 2015*

Appendix J
Entry #55
Lending Library

"Starting a Parish Lending Library" *By John W. Truslow, Jr.*
This article is written in the hope that you, with God's help, will pray for and build a parish/mission lending library for the good of your own community and for your own edification as well. Enough details will be set forth so that you can actually get started with the information given to you. Consider these central propositions:

First: Parish lending libraries are one significant part of the life-long, generation-after-generation discipleship ministry of the Orthodox Church with the great objective of deification — by God's grace with our cooperation — for every person.

Second: Lending libraries are easy and fun to create and to operate continually in a parish or mission, but only if three key rules are continually observed in practice: *Keep it Small, Simple, and Spiritual* (KISSS for ease of memory).

Third: If the parish priest and his parish council are in conscious agreement with the above and if one or two parishioners are initially willing to act in accord with that willingness, then a lending library can start within three months.

Nine years ago in the adult education classes in the parish where I am a member, someone said, "You know we could all learn more about the Faith if we had good Orthodox materials readily available to us here. We ought to have a parish library." About two dozen people said, "Amen! What a great idea!" It was four years after that comment before we could actually start a library largely because: (1) we had trouble articulating the reasons for a library to others; (2) we had no shared concept of what operational principals should guide us toward the right kind of library for an Orthodox parish; and, (3) quite reasonably, given (1) and (2), the priest and council regularly saw other needs as having priority over a library.

Once we agreed on the basic concepts set forth in this article, we were in operation loaning good Orthodox materials to the faithful within three months. And now, over five years later, we are still loaning 400 items a year on average in a parish with 187 households. We have reached our design goal of 500 Orthodox items and continue to focus upon constantly encouraging our fellow parishioners to use these materials. Almost any willing parish/mission can have a parish lending library in operation within a calendar quarter. I've seen this actually happen successfully in a mission not far from our parish.

Two things about the word *library* need saying here. First parish/mission lending libraries simply must not be seen as being comparable or in competition with either of the following:

(a) seminary libraries with all their many obligations and objectives including research and scholarly publication; or,

(b) public libraries with their incredible apparent mandate to be all things to all interest groups in the general body politic.

Second, the word *library* (from the Latin word for book) today communicates not so much the format (which narrowly could mean just "books") but rather the idea of assistance in access to Orthodox information which may be 80% books and 20% "other" formats such as Orthodox music CDs, CD-ROMs, audio cassette tapes, video tapes, internet providers, etc.

What then is a lending library appropriate to the needs of an Orthodox Christian parish or mission? Let's reconsider proposition number one.

We — like the twelve Disciples — are "in training" as we fellow Christ in His Church. Our ultimate objective is "deification" or the restoration, by God's grace, of the image and likeness of God in us. Orthodoxy holds as true the idea that we are to cooperate our whole lives with God in achieving this objective. There are many proper ways to be doing this, of which a lending library is just one — but it is one! Christ read and we imitate Him.

Next we should consider what guidelines will best describe the functioning of a library which will best serve this general discipleship objective. To do this we may review our second proposition.

This KISSS device is a way to keep the parish lending library on the right track "forever" as it faces many unpredictable situations.

Small means you need not have much space and often no available "extra room with 4 walls." Small means that you can start and maintain a really good library with 150-200 paperback Orthodox books in an attractive lockable cabinet sitting on a sturdy dolly with castors (both available at your office supply store). When the floor must be waxed or space needed desperately for a parish festival, no problem. The library is simply rolled off into a corner until the excitement dies down. To expand just buy a second cabinet.

If you are a mission in rented space having to set up each Sunday, you too could have a lending library. Aim for 50 paperbacks in a small foot locker carried in for the fellowship hour after Divine Liturgy on Sunday. The point is that every parish/mission needs a Library; do not let fantasies of what a library "should be" keep you from doing what you can do given your present facilities.

But, right from the beginning, you need self-imposed size limits for your library. You must control collection growth because you library can easily get out of hand over time and become too big for the other competing, legitimate needs for space. A mission renting space for Sundays with 25 households and a "movable footlocker library" should hold the size down to 50-75 items. The mission with 50 households and its own space for a "rolling cabinet" should hold the collection to about 150-200 items. The small-to-medium parish with 100-200 households may have 5 cabinets and 500-750 items. Even large parishes should have clear limits. Think *small* for success!

No effective parish lending library is ever merely a warehouse for books. You want a library with a relatively small collection that is really being used (10-15% should be out on loan at all times.) Weekly ads in the Sunday bulletin, posters promoting reading, and personal persuasion of members of the congregation will help keep circulation high. A huge collection with 1% in circulation is a net waste of resources. And, if you get too big, you can become intimidating.

Another reason for a small lending library is so it can be deliberately placed "in the way" of the parishioners. The best place is often near the coffee pots where the people gather for fellowship. A small library (relative to your parish size) with good Orthodox books actually being lent and read is the ideal!

Simplicity is possible for you, whereas it would be an absolute disaster for the larger, multi-disciplinary library. You have no need for a complex book classification system when your library is essentially about one discipline called "Orthodoxy." You can have virtually all your books in alphabetical order on the shelves by the first important word (skipping *a*, *an*, and *the*) in the spine title. However, books for youth and children are often better held in their own section and organized by shelves for the different ages/grades.

Circulation of materials means that what goes out must come back in. While not attended the library must be locked up or otherwise secured or else you will soon not have a library at all. The books will all be in the homes of well-meaning people who certainly intended to bring them back, but who just forgot. A simple three-part (white, yellow, pink) pressure sensitive form can be printed at your local office supply store to serve as a loan card. Everyone who borrows a book is helped to fill out the form with his name, day and evening phone numbers, the title and author of the item, the volume number, copy number, and acquisition cost (data which can be conveniently noted on the title page of each book), what month it is being borrow and the next following month (which is the month of return). The idea is to give busy people a full month or more to get the book read.

The three-part forms are used this way: the top (white) copy and the yellow (second) copies are filed (stuck together) in a loan card box behind a tab for the month the book is due, e.g. "September" (a book loaned out anytime in August is due back anytime in September). The pink (third) copy is placed inside the book at the time of borrowing to remind the borrower what month it is due back to the library. The pink copy is left in the book by the borrower when it is returned to the "Book Return Box" in the library. A big "X" may be drawn through the white copy which is placed behind a "returned books" tab in the "Loan Card File Box" as a permanent record of circulation for that calendar year. Only then is the book re-shelved.

But what if the book doesn't come back by the end of September? The yellow copy is pulled off the white copy, given to and used by the library's "repo man" helper to get the book back by calling to remind the borrower to return the book once every week until the book is returned. Lost or destroyed books must be replaced or paid for by the borrower. Persistence is crucial to library survival.

Spiritual. Not just any "spirituality" will do since we are limited ourselves to Orthodox parish lending libraries. Anything "outside" of the Holy Orthodox Faith has to be kept "outside" the lending library. Keeping heretical materials out is surprisingly difficult over time. That is why every single book given to the library or suggested for library purchase must be pre-approved by the priest. The delay that this will entail is well worth the benefit of keeping the library Orthodox and not "something else."

Also, non-spiritual items unrelated to Holy Orthodoxy must be kept out of the Orthodox parish lending library lest the library turn into a sad attempt with totally insufficient resources to duplicate the local public library collection. A parish lending library can really do only one thing well: provide good, solid, spiritual Orthodox materials to Orthodox people who seek deification with God's help. If the parish library can do that one thing it will have done well.

One of the best initial sources of materials for starting parish libraries is simply to let every household in the parish know that a library is being started and ask for the contribution of Orthodox books (with the usual condition of the automatic review by the priest). The truth is that a well-run library allows us to share our books with each other so they don't gather dust on our shelves at home after one reading. If we ever want to read "our: book again, the library will loan it to us. Good stewardship includes having 24 people read one book instead of just the purchaser. Sharing books just makes good sense.

Besides request for gifts of "used books" from parishioners, the other way to acquire books and materials is by purchase. Thankfully, there are several Orthodox publishers in English now. Initially you just need to know that Saint Vladimir's Seminary bookstore has two excellent services: (1) SVS will sell your parish an "instant library" (called "packages") of 50 to 150 Orthodox paperback books in English at a reasonable price; and (2) SVS has the Press Club, a subscription to which will result in your library receiving a few newly-published Orthodox books every couple of months. Also, Conciliar Press has a display rack and starter set especially for visitors and inquirers of topical booklets and brochures. The library is the perfect parish support center for low-key, personal Orthodox evangelism to visitors and inquirers.

The third and last proposition is: If the parish priest and his parish council are in conscious agreement with the above and if one or two parishioners are initially willing to act in accord with that willingness then a lending library can start within three months.

The parish lending library must be perceived as being "owned" by the whole parish and a normal part of the parish discipleship program. The priest and the council need to agree that a lending library is desirable for the parish. Assuming agreement on a need for a library, the parish council should authorize a special account ("the Library Fund") to receive and expand both annually budgeting and specially offered money under the supervision of the parish treasurer.

About half of the annual cost should be funded in the budget and the other half by individual designated offerings. This will automatically place the library and its finances under whatever audit programs exist and enhance the credibility of the library. The bottom line cost of starting is currently $10 or $12 a paperback on average or about $500 for the "footlocker library" and from $1000 to $2000 for the "rolling cabinet(s) library."

If there is a parish bookstore, the library may elect to buy books at cost from t and thereby enjoy the 20% trade discount from publishers. Again, for any cooperation to occur, the priest and the council must encourage it by seeing both bookstore and library as being compatible ways of encouraging discipleship throughout the parish.

The first continuing priestly role in supporting the library is in his prior approval of library materials. The other continuing priestly role is in helping to identify those with talents from God to work on the library team. Two Library Coordinators may head up the overall effort. One coordinator may work on development of the collection (finance, acquisition, culling, physical plant) and the other on circulation (including library marketing, repossessing of overdue items, shelving and recruiting helpers).

To avoid burnout, helpers who open up the Library after worship should serve in rotation only once every two months (e.g. "Bill serves second Sundays of Even Months"). Helpers on duty should be identifiable by a pinned-on blue ribbon with "LIBRARY" printed on it (available from the office supply store). Remind helpers of duty dates, train them and say "thanks" regularly.

Why not start your parish lending library this calendar quarter? Questions? Please write St Elias Antiochian Orthodox Church, ATTN: Lending Library, 2045 Ponce de Leon Ave. NE, Atlanta, Georgia 30307.

John W. Truslow, Jr. is Coordinator of the Library Ministry Team at St Elias.

This article was reprinted from *Word Magazine* dated December 2001.

Appendix K
Entry #77
Guest Speaker Topics

Speakers Available by Topic

- Abortion (3)
- Academia (1)
- Addiction (1)
- Adventure (1)
- Akathistos Hymn (1)
- American Culture (10)
- Animal Rights (1)
- Anthropology (3)
- Arab Culture (1)
- Art (7)
- Bereavement (1)
- Biblical Studies (4)
- Bioethics (1)
- Byzantine Art (3)
- Byzantine Chant (1)
- Celtic Christianity (1)
- Charity (1)
- Children (1)
- Chronic Disease Prevention (1)
- Church & State (2)
- Church Calendar (2)
- Church Fathers (1)
- Cinema (1)
- Cloning (1)
- Cloning (human) (1)
- Communication (2)
- Comparative Religions (3)
- Conversion (4)
- Crisis Ministry (1)
- Cults (1)
- Cultural Understanding (2)
- Cultural War (4)
- Culture (2)
- Death (1)
- Divine Liturgy (2)
- Ecclesiology (3)
- Ecology (4)
- Ecumenism (1)
- Education (4)
- Environmentalism (1)
- Eschatology (3)
- Ethics (5)
- Ethics (Legal) (1)
- Ethics (Medical) (1)
- Euthanasia (3)
- Evangelism (3)
- Evolution (2)
- Family (9)
- Fatherhood (1)
- Feminism (1)
- Forgiveness (1)
- Free-Masonry (1)
- Gender & Sexuality (3)
- Global warming (1)
- Government (3)
- Government & Law (2)
- Great Canon of St. Andrew (1)
- Great Lent (1)
- Harry Potter (1)
- Health (1)
- Health and Nutrition (1)
- Health and Well-Being (2)
- Healthcare Reform (1)
- Heresies (1)
- Heterodoxy (1)
- History - Art (2)
- History - Church (8)
- History - Scriptures (1)
- Holistic Health (1)
- Holy Tradition (3)
- Home Schooling (1)
- Hymnography (1)
- Icons (5)
- Infant Death (1)
- Infertility (1)
- Intelligent Design and Evolution (2)
- Intercultural Marriage (1)
- Interpreting the Bible and the Constitution (1)
- Investigative Services (1)
- Journalism (1)
- Leadership (1)
- Life Abroad (1)
- Literature (5)
- Liturgical Practices (2)
- Liturgical Theology (6)
- Marriage (7)
- Martyrdom (2)
- Medicine (1)

- Ministerial Misconduct (1)
- Miracles (1)
- Miscarriage (1)
- Motherhood (1)
- Mount Athos (1)
- Natural Law (1)
- Nature of Man (1)
- Nature of the Church (2)
- Non-Violence (2)
- Nutrition (1)
- Orthodox Praxis (13)
- Orthodox Tradition (7)
- OSB (1)
- Outreach (1)
- Parenting (5)
- Parish Life (2)
- Pascha (1)
- Peace (1)
- Persecution (2)
- Poetry (3)
- Politics (5)
- Pop Culture (1)
- Prayer (6)
- Psychiatry (1)
- Public Affairs (1)
- Relational Theology (1)
- Religion in the News (1)
- Romantic Relationships (2)
- Sacramental Living (7)
- Sacramental Theology (3)
- Sacraments (1)
- Safety and Security (1)
- Saints (4)
- Same-sex Marriage (1)
- Sanctity of Life (1)
- Science & Theology (2)
- Sexual Abuse (2)
- Sexuality (1)
- Slavs (1)
- Social Justice (1)
- Spiritual Warfare (1)
- St. John Chysostom (1)
- Stem Cell Research (3)
- Suffering (3)
- Symbol of Faith (1)
- Technology/New Media (5)
- The Apocalypse (1)
- the Constitution (1)
- The Holy Spirit (1)
- The Holy Trinity (1)
- The Ladder of Divine Ascent (1)
- the Law of War (1)
- The Theotokos (1)
- Ukraine (1)
- Vocation (1)
- War (1)
- Weight Loss (2)
- Weight Management (2)
- Welfare (1)
- Wellness (1)
- Womanhood (1)
- Women's health (1)
- Work (1)
- World Religions (1)
- Worship (2)
- Writing (2)
- Youth (1)
- Youth Ministry (2)

Appendix L
Entry #85
Prison Ministry

Ideas for Prison Ministry Awareness Sunday Homilies – May 17, 2015

Epistle Reading: Acts of the Apostles 16:16-34 *"Having received this charge, he put them into the inner prison and fastened their feet in the stocks. But about midnight Paul and Silas were praying and singing hymns to God, and the prisoners were listening to them, and suddenly there was a great earthquake, so that the foundations of the prison were shaken; and immediately all the doors were opened and every one's fetters were unfastened."*

Men and women in prison are bound up with much more than bars and restraints. Their lives have been shattered and they have become bound up with their own sins and with their own thoughts. OCPM sends prayer books into these precious souls. These prayer books cover all the daily prayers, including the midnight prayers. One Hierarch, after visited the men in a maximum secure prison, commented that "some of their prayer lives put mine to shame!" These men were praying all of the daily prayers in the OCPM Prayer Book.

"Believe in the Lord Jesus, and you will be saved, you and your household."

The ministry of OCPM reaches beyond the men and women in prison, touching even the lives of some of their families. The people in prison tell their families about their new found Faith and the families begin exploring it for themselves. Some OCPM books find their way right into the homes of the precious families. When one person comes to the Orthodox Faith, all those who see him or her are also impacted by the Lord and His Church.

Gospel Reading: John 9:1-38 *"At that time, as Jesus passed by, he saw a man blind from his birth."*

Many of the people in prison have been spiritually blind their whole lives. They are often school dropouts from broken and dysfunctional families, whose lives have been ones of continual abuse. God has a heart for these precious people in prison and He seems to reach out to them in amazing ways. The Theotokos and other Saints have appeared to some of the toughest or the tough prisoners in order to soften their hearts and open their blind eyes.

"It was not that this man sinned, or his parents, but that the works of God might be made manifest in him. We must work the works of him who sent me, while it is day; night comes, when no one can work. As long as I am in the world, I am the light of the world."

It is still day and we must work the works of the Lord on this earth. Christ came to bring the Light to these precious souls living in darkness and He calls all of us to be a part of this work. "I was in prison and you visited me!" Not all of us can go into a prison, but all of us can be involved with prison ministry. We can help send prayer and study books to them; we can help send Holy Icons to them; we can help with the training of those who will go into the prisons or those who will write people in prison. Our gifts today will make us a part of the wonderful ministry of OCPM. Night is coming; let us work while we can!

"Go, wash in the pool of Siloam" (which means Sent). So he went and washed and came back seeing."

Can you imagine in your mind what this blind man must have felt when his eyes were opened? That same joy fills the heart of every man and woman in prison who is baptized into the Holy Orthodox Faith or who returns to the Faith of their youth. (Former altar boys have come back to the Church in prison! Their spiritual eyes are opened and their lives are transformed. One man who was baptized in a maximum secure prison wept through his entire baptism.

Appendix M
Entry #98
Orthodox Natural Church Development

"Reclaiming the Gospel" *by Bradley Nassif*

Most of my life's work over the past fifty-one years has been devoted to understanding God's truth as it has been known in the Orthodox tradition. I completed four advanced degrees in New Testament, European History, Orthodox pastoral studies, and my doctoral work in patristics under the late Fr. John Meyendorff. I've been an invited speaker at prestigious conferences around the world, done television documentaries, taught at leading seminaries, and published widely. All this, however, means absolutely nothing if I do not keep the Person of Christ at the very center of my life and thought. Without Him, I am an ignorant theologian -a big zero!

The same is true for our Orthodox churches in America and abroad. I am convinced that the Orthodox Church preserves the fullness of God's truth, but I am equally persuaded that we have not made that truth meaningful and accessible to our own Church members. The most urgent need in the Orthodox world today is the need for an aggressive "internal mission" of (re)converting our people to Jesus Christ. The gospel of Christ and our life in Him need to be reclaimed as the very centerpiece of Church life.

A Lament Over Unchanged Lives: We all know that the Orthodox Church possesses a very rich and beautiful theological inheritance. Few would dispute the architectural wonder of our cathedrals, the artistic beauty of our iconography, or the inspirational impact of our ancient hymns and liturgical services. Our theological literature from the past continues to define the meaning of the word orthodoxy for those who have lost their way in the contemporary maze of theological liberalism, cultic religion, or postmodernism. We Orthodox have done better than all others at "not changing the faith once delivered to the saints" (Jude 1:3).

Still, it is quite obvious from the weak participation in our liturgical services and in the personal lives of some members, that Orthodoxy is often failing to meet the spiritual needs of our people -- in America as well as the motherlands of Russia, Greece, Eastern Europe and the Middle East. Parishioners are coming and going in and out of church with little visible change in their lives. In short, they do not know the core content of the gospel or how to integrate its meaning into their everyday lives. I realize these are sad things to say, but a correct diagnosis precedes the proper cure.

Are Our People Evangelized or Sacramentalized? What I'm sayi[ng is that] contemporary Orthodoxy possesses the gospel in a formal way but [not] translating it in a relevant, life-changing way. The clarity of the go[spel is not] intentionally made central to our liturgical services and every[day life.] Formally, in its liturgy, sacraments, iconography, hymnography, spirituality, and theological literature, the Orthodox Church is extremely Christ-centered; in practice, however, it is not. Just because the gospel is formally in the life of the Church does not mean that Orthodox parishioners have understood and appropriated its message! Our bishops and priests need to make the gospel crystal clear and absolutely central in our parishes.

This is not to say sermons are not preached. They are, and are often eloquent. But very often what priests preach are not the life, death, and resurrection of Jesus and His call to total commitment and what that means to everyday life and liturgy. Our leaders wrongly assume everybody knows about that subject. Instead of Christ-centered messages, we hear sermons dealing with moral values, social issues, financial giving, the environment, or the need for more Church attendance -all inseparably related to the gospel, but not to be confused with the Good News itself. In effect, the authentic gospel is replaced with a social gospel or a liturgical gospel (as if simply "going to Church" is all that is needed). I often wonder, "Are our people really evangelized, or are they simply sacramentalized?"

True sacramental preaching makes the gospel central to every liturgical act and every liturgical season of fasting and prayer. Without the centrality of the gospel we end up imposing on our people the evil of religious formalism and barren ritualism. It is, in effect, not a true Orthodoxy but a false Orthodoxy. Bishops and priests must not take for granted that everyone in the Church is converted and has no need to hear the basic gospel message. The life-changing message of the forgiveness of sins and new life in Christ must be deliberately applied to the entire sacramental life of the Church. Christ-centered preaching and Christ-centered worship must be faithfully performed by our priests and bishops if they wish to worship God truly in "spirit and in truth" (John 4).

Focus on the Centrality of "Christ," not the Centrality of "Orthodoxy": Outside of Orthodoxy, have you noticed how the healthiest Christian communities around today are the ones who preach Christ, not their own denomination? They speak of Jesus, not their "Baptist," "Methodist" or "Pentecostal" identities. Yet, all we seem to hear from our pulpits is "Orthodoxy, Orthodoxy, Orthodoxy!" We are obsessed with self-definition through negation. It is a sick religious addiction. We often shore up our identity as Orthodox by constantly contrasting ourselves with Evangelicals or Catholics. I wish we would talk more about Christian faith, and less about "Orthodoxy."

As a theologian, I know full well that differences do matter and that it is important for our parishioners to be aware of them. But we must not let our religious environment dictate the emphases of our spiritual lives. I wonder how many priests and people can go a full year without talking about how "different" they are from one of their Protestant or Catholic brethren? Our sister churches in the Patriarchate of Antioch throughout the Middle East seem to do a much better job at this than we do in America. They have learned to live peacefully with their fellow non-Orthodox Christians and Muslims without constantly resorting to the fundamentalism of an Orthodox jihad! Today, however, we in America get bent out of shape if the priest wants to invite a non-Orthodox speaker or encourage Bible studies with fellow conservative Christians. Yet priests do it frequently in the Middle East.

Consider this single proposition: If the gospel is made clearer and more central to all we do in the Church, we will truly be Orthodox in reality and not in name only. I am not trying to be simplistic or reductionistic; on the contrary, I am seeking to be faithful to the maximalist vision of the faith of the Eastern Orthodox Church. Christ is the Alpha and the Omega, the beginning and the end of all things, and the cure for all our sins and weaknesses.

Be that as it may, numerous consequences result from self-consciously making the gospel clearer and more central to our Church life. Once Jesus, in His trinitarian relations, is proclaimed in all the Church's sacraments and liturgical actions, then the Church's preaching, worship, missions, and education will reflect that Christ-centeredness. For example:

- Worship services will be more meaningful because the priest shows how Christ heals us through the different sacraments.
- The Divine Liturgy will not focus on the Eucharist "per se," but on Christ in the liturgy of the Word and in the liturgy of the sacrament, two inseparable aspects of the Sunday liturgy.
- Christian education will not simply be about learning the symbolic meaning of the priest's vestments, Church architecture, etc., but about the Bible itself and how Jesus Christ and the Holy Trinity are the primary focus of those vestments and artistic expressions of theology.
- The Church's missionary work will not simply seek to "plant churches," but to "convert sinners" to personal faith in Christ through repentance, faith, and baptism. Moreover, its internal mission to parishioners who are Orthodox in name only may, for the first time, lead people into a saving relationship with Christ through rededicating their lives to the Lord as a renewal of their baptism.
- Finally, in the Church's preaching, the gospel of Jesus Christ will be applied to the marketplace of business, school, social, and family life.

Quite simply, we need to recover the evangelical dimensions of our Church's faith (see my chapter, "The Evangelical Theology of the Eastern Orthodox Church" in *Three Views on Eastern Orthodoxy and Evangelicalism*, ed. James Stamoolis, Zondervan, 2004). We need to make the pulpit agree with the altar. Strange as it may sound, the Church's preaching needs to become more Eucharistic. Why? Because the Eucharist proclaims the gospel! It "proclaims the Lord's death, until He comes." The death, resurrection and second coming of Christ are the very core of the Good News.

Be Clear About the Gospel and Make it the Core of Your Life and Ministry: The Orthodox Church has such a long history and rich theology that it is easy for us to lose sight of the forest for the trees. But we must never lose sight of the simplicity of the gospel and its far-reaching consequences for everyday life. That is why I am so concerned to relate the Church's faith to the work-a-day-world of the common Christian. I have offered weekend seminars at churches on "Desert Spirituality for City Folk" in an attempt to translate the principles of monastic life (not their lifestyle) to the spiritual disciplines of the average Christian (fasting, prayer, meditation, Bible reading). I also teach a college course titled "Selling with Soul!" for helping Christian businessmen integrate their faith in the marketplace. I believe that the same sort of thing can be done in all our parishes if we keep our eyes on the cultural relevance of the gospel.

So, in the end, if we Orthodox wish to possess a truly incarnational, trinitarian faith, we will constantly need to recover the personal and relational aspects of God in every life-giving action of the Church. Failure to keep the gospel central will constitute an experiential denial of our own faith. We must stop our religious addiction to "Orthodoxy" and its "differences" with the West. We need rather to recover the evangelical dimensions of our total Church life. The liturgy itself exhorts us to that end. The four Gospels are the only books that sit upon the very center of the altar because in them alone do we hear the Good News -- all else in the Church is commentary. It is the Bible which guides and judges the Church, not the other way around. Thus, in the words of St. John Chrysostom, whose name our liturgy bears, "The lack of Scriptural knowledge is the source of all evils in the Church." I fear that many converts are coming to the Church through a revolving door, quietly leaving because their lives and families are not being sufficiently fed. Only a gospel-transformation will make the Orthodox Church healthy enough to sustain the lives of parishioners who seek spiritual nourishment in our communities.

Bradley Nassif, Ph.D. is from St. Mary's Orthodox Church in Wichita, KS and Holy Transfiguration Antiochian Orthodox Church, Warrenville, IL. He is Professor of Biblical and Theological Studies, North Park University (Chicago); editor of New Perspectives on Historical Theology: Essays in *(Eerdmans, 1996); and author of the forthcoming Westminster Handbook to Eastern Orthodox Theology(Westminster John Knox Press, 2008). He may be reached at* bnassif@northpark.edu.

About The Author

Adam Lowell Roberts lives in Franklin, TN with his wife, three children, and a cat which proves aliens exist. When Adam is not writing, he is usually laughing at his own jokes or being told he is too loud. Adam's favorite quote is, "behind every great man is a woman rolling her eyes."

You can contact Adam in the following ways.

Website/Blog: www.adamlowellroberts.com

Facebook: www.facebook.com/adamlowellroberts

Podcast: goforth@ancientfaith.com

Made in the USA
San Bernardino, CA
20 August 2016